FREE TO BE...ME

CRISTI R. WILLIAMS

Relax, Recline, & Read
Texarkana, TX

RRR
Relax, Recline, & Read
2801 Richmond Road 369
Texarkana, TX 75503

Designed by Nesi Writes

Manufactured in the United States of America

Free to Be...Me/Cristi R. Williams.
1. Self-Improvement. 2. Spirituality. 3. Christianity
4. Williams, Cristi R.
I. Title

ISBN-13: 978-1456539672
ISBN-10: 1456539671

TRAPPED BUT FREE

I'm racing, searching for a place to hide—strangled by strongholds binding me. Where do I go to escape these haunting deeds choking me? I'm trapped inside myself—there's nowhere to flee. Where do I go to hide from this image of myself when this is all I know? I'm blinded by the scene. I'm trapped. However, I'm free.

Time stands still, yet, it moves. The pace, intermingled with the ticking of the swift and slow pressures of life, engulfs me as tidal waves crash over me—refreshing and relaxing, horrific as well as terrifying. There's no life for me.

In this tunnel of despair, light awaits. I feel warmth and a strong embrace. I'm home—trapped. However, I am free.

When will this confusing duality end?

When will these battle wounds cease?

I'm searching for a consistent life—one never changing where my mind meets my spirit, where the kiss of peace seals the agreement immersing me in holy matrimony to walk in the power of unity within myself.

For now, my tears flow into rivers deep—full of sadness and hope. Nevertheless, in this chaotic state, I find joy in knowing there is so much more.

But, presently, I'm trapped, yet, free almost free to be…FREE TO BE ME!

FREEDOM

Do you feel free enough to exercise your choices in a way pleasing to you?

Are you a person who knows what it's like to think for yourself without worrying what others say or think about you?

Many have learned to break out of the molds of conformity—marching to their own drum beat without fear of retribution, punishment, and the pressures of social groups, family, friends, church folks, etc.

Let me paint a picture for you.

As a human being, you have the individual right to think freely, express your thoughts, and opinions.

You are free to assemble peacefully, associate with others, join groups for the protection of your interests, and shape how you want to live your life.

You also have security rights protecting you against crimes like murder, massacre, torture, and rape.

Your freedom gives you due process rights that protect you against legal system abuse like imprisonment without trial, secret trials, and excessive punishments.

Freedom gives you liberty—protecting your beliefs, expression, associations, assembly, and movement.

You are free.

With your freedom, you're entitled to social and welfare rights requiring education provision and protections against severe poverty and starvation.

In the United States, you have basic human rights protecting you against abuses of your dignity and your fundamental interests.

You're free to have a good life, to move about— finding the necessities of life, pursuing your own plans for living and maintaining ties to your family and friends if you so choose.

However, some of us are in such bondage and oppression because we don't know *who* we are, *what* we are, or *why* we are here so we can operate in our freedom.

I hope to shine some light that will give you invaluable information to help you on your journey to freely be yourself.

Some of us perish because we lack knowledge.

We're immobilized when it comes to being who we are, doing what we want, and living our lives as we wish.

Today I proclaim again, *"Let freedom ring'*. I've been bound myself.

Daily I'm learning to walk more in my freedom.

I've learned that the real truth of freedom is staying in the boundaries of God.

With the knowledge of knowing that I'm free to be me,

I invite you to join me on this freedom walk discovering *who* you are, *what* you are, and *why* you exist.

Examples of Freedom

- You enjoy rights and liberty as a person not in enslaved.

- You're exempt from external authority, interference, and restriction to be yourself.

- You're independent—autonomous.

- You exercise your ability to do things of your choosing—at will, and fearlessly take action.

- You're free from worry the majority of the time.

- You feel safe—free from danger.

- You have the freedom to enter places at will and to enjoy yourself.

- You're released from physical and inward bondage, imprisonment, and restraint.

- You're released from ties and obligations hindering you from being your true self.

If your life doesn't match any or the majority of the things listed above which paint a picture of freedom, hopefully something mentioned in the following pages will help set you free to be you.

<u>Acknowledgments</u>

I give all glory to my Lord and Savior, Jesus Christ.
Thank you for entrusting me to carry this word in my womb and allowing me to birth it into existence. I am forever humbled and grateful.

I thank my husband, Greg Williams, for loving and supporting every endeavor God places within me.
Honey, you are my ministry, and I love you.

I thank my family—my Mom and sisters for love unconditionally, and my deceased grandparents, Aravine & Alma Stovall for leaving the impression of Christ in and on my heart.

I thank my editor, Nesi Writes, and my publisher, *Relax, Recline, & Read,* for molding and shaping "Baby".

Thank you to all my friends and supporters in my sphere of influence for accepting my breath. I am now able to believe in myself. I Am *FREE to BE…ME*

INTRODUCTION

When darkness comes gripping my soul and stillness blackens the night, I lay waiting for signals of help.

Instead, I'm deafened by the echoes of my cries.

This swirling tunnel encases me.

I'm floating, turning, moving, and shifting through the movement of time.

My birth is at hand.

My stay is but for a fleeting moment—for earth cannot contain me.

Contamination, pain, heartache, and shadows feel foreign to my *true* identity.

I sigh because the journey I am about to take is necessary.

Upon entering this world, I ask, "*Who* am I to be? *What* am I to do? *Why* am I here?"

These questions haunt every human's soul in the midst of doubt and uncertainty.

A sense of assuredness envelops me.

I'm free-falling—tumbling thinking no one will catch me.

However, I am supported by unseen hands leading, guiding, and pushing me through the birth canal to be myself.

I'm panting, sweating, and pushing through the cries of labor's travail.

The world awaits my delivery as heaven applauds what humans have yet to see.

I have landed in this present time and space.

My assignment awaits me positioning me for places I must sojourn—living as *who* I'm to be, expressing *what* I'm to do, and experiencing *why* I'm here.

I'm a vapor, a mist, a breath in this realm called earth.

Those I'm to influence received my birth announcement that states, "I am FREE to BE…ME!"

I dedicate this book to my three daughters,

LaKelya, LaChelya, and Kali

Embrace your true identity
Eradicate the mistakes of your past
Evolve into the expression of your spirit
You are FREE to BE…

FREE TO BE...ME

WHO AM I?

We've heard this question asked many times as we've traveled this life's journey, "Who are you?"

We've even asked ourselves, "Who am I?"

May I ask you, dear friend, "Who are you?"

Before you answer, think about the question.

I don't want to know your name. I don't want to know your profession.

I want to know you—the *real* you.

When women are asked who they are, we commonly respond by giving our name or telling someone that I'm the wife of···, I'm the mother of···, I'm a nurse, I work at···, etc.

We generally equate who we are with our connections.

You're not your name, the people you're connected to, or even the things you do.

Who you are flows much deeper than that.

Your parents gave you your name to distinguish you from other people in the world. But, something much deeper identifies who you really are.

It's called your *spirit.*

That's right. You read correctly.

Go ahead and say it out loud. *Spirit*!

You're a spirit-being housed in a body to accomplish a designated purpose that was predetermined for you before you were born.

The spirit living inside of you is who you are.

No, I mean the *real* you—the true you.

For a lot of us, our spirit is the part of us that has yet to be tapped into.

Your spirit is the side of you that's not been fully discovered—the hidden part of you. The part of you that is full of dreams and desires.

Your spirit needs an awakening so you can experience life—not just survive—to be fully you.

When God formed Adam, he was just that—a form.

A form is a framework of an entity.

Your body is your form.

The Bible states in Genesis 2:7, "And the Lord God *formed* Adam out of the dust of the ground···"

God formed Adam. He structured Adam. He gave Adam an outward shape—a body relatable to the conceptual view God perceived him to be.

See, God is sovereign. He's all powerful and all knowing. He is the Creator.

When He created and creates, He already has the awareness in His mind of what a thing is to be.

Let me free you up a bit right here by telling you that your body—the form of you, the structure of you, and the shape of you—was predetermined before you were born.

So, stop worrying about the shape of your thighs, stressing about the shape of your nose, crying over this and that because it's just the form of you that God chose to house the real you—your spirit.

Everything about Adam's body was already predetermined, laid out beforehand—from the size of his head to the name he would be given.

It was preordained by God.

It's the same with us.

It doesn't matter your nationality, gender, or the socio-economic status you're rolling in because honestly, it's really not who you are.

My form is African-American, but, my spirit isn't.

My form is a woman, but, my spirit isn't. Society calls me middle-class, but, my spirit isn't.

My essence isn't African-American. I am spirit.

My true-self isn't a woman. I am spirit.

My soul isn't middle-class. I am spirit.

I ask you again, "Who are you?"

You are a *spirit.*

When God wanted Adam to be manifested on this earth, He formed him out of the dust of the earth. God shaped and molded a body for Adam.

But, can I tell you something?

Adam existed long before he was formed—glory to God!

Adam already had life because he was inside of God.

When God wanted man to come forth on the earth, He sculpted and shaped the form He had in mind that would be an image of Himself—a representation of God on earth.

Like I said, after God molded and sculpted Adam, he was just a form.

He was simply a shape in preparation of becoming a living soul.

The Bible specifies that God breathed into Adam's nostrils the breath of life and Adam became a living soul.

Adam went from being a form to being *spirit*, a living soul, when God breathed into him.

Adam went from being a lifeless mold to a life-filled being.

When God breathed into Adam, He breathed Himself into him.

Everything that was of God was deposited on the inside of Adam.

What do you mean, Cristi?

I mean that God's breath *is* God. God's breath *is* Spirit. God's breath *is* Life.

So, when God wanted a replica of Himself manifested in the earth-realm, He formed a man, breathed life into his nostrils, and named him Adam.

We need God's breath so our spirit—our essence, our true being—can live and breathe.

We need air so our forms—our bodies—can function on this earth.

There's no way we can live or breathe without God's breath.

God breathed the breath of life into the nostrils of man.

As I studied, I asked God this question.

"God, why is it that you breathed into the nostrils of man and not into his mouth? To me, it makes more sense that the mouth would be where you breathed your breath."

God said, *"I didn't breathe into the mouth of man because I was not giving him mouth-to-mouth resuscitation. I wasn't reviving him. I was breathing (birthing) life into him."*

Many of us are simply forms, molds, going through the motions of living, merely surviving.

Since we behave as if life is not in us, we end up in places DOA (Dead on Arrival) because we don't know who we are.

This is not the plan God has preordained for us.

So, go to your mirror.

Take a look and ask yourself this question again.

"Who Am I—the real me?"

You are not the person your father and momma, siblings, teachers, friends, co-workers, etc. say you are.

Who are you?

You are not the spouse you married, the children you birthed, the job where you work, or the church you attend.

Who are you?

You are not the pianist, the usher, the preacher, or the prophet.

Who are you?

You are not a victim, abuse, shame, guilt, condemnation, or any other demeaning label.

Some untrue labels are wrapped around, stuck on, pressed into, and fused into us trying to communicate to people their perception of the content inside of our packaging.

It's time to disconnect from untruthful labels directing our lives.

We were created to live out of our spirit—who we are—not by misappropriated labels used to define us.

I can tell you, a lot of labels convey that additives

have been mixed in diluting the real thing—tainting the genuine product.

Circumstances, the enemy of our soul, and the world system are notorious for adding contaminants that taint us.

Labels like depression, suicide, fornication, etc. are very poisonous additives poured into us—mocking us, stealing from us, killing us, and destroying us.

These additives are mixed into us to snuff out our true identity.

You are *spirit.*

You don't need improving.

You don't need worldly or satanically influenced additives to be who you truly are because you are from God.

You're complete in your spirit.

So go ahead, right now, take you a praise break to give God glory.

While you're giving Him glory, release those

additives designed to make you less than you are, unleash all those counterfeit accessories.

Then tell the world and the devil, "These additives do not define who I am. Shame is too tight. Shacking is too little. I have outgrown gossip. I can't wear this fake stuff anymore. I wasn't designed for it."

Now that you've disrobed and are naked before God, you don't have to be ashamed.

Your designer original garment is just waiting to fashion you. So, get up, go, and slip into your *spirit* because that is the *real* you.

Genesis 1:27 states, "So God created man in His *own* image; in the image of God He created him; male and female He created them."

The word, *create*, means to bring into existence, to produce.

The word *image* means a reproduction, a prototype, a duplicate.

When someone takes a picture of you, it's a replica

of you.

The picture is a reproduction, a copy, a representation of you.

It's not a fake.

The image shows what you look like.

No one sat in your place pretending to be you.

So, when the picture develops, and you look at it, you see a likeness of how you are reflected in the world.

Sometimes we see pictures of ourselves and are shocked at what we see—the weight gain, the wrinkles, bags under the eyes, or whatever.

Then we say, "I hate taking pictures. I'm just not photogenic."

Well, I beg to differ. I think you are very photogenic.

I just think the lens focused, captured, snapped, and exposed you.

Sometimes there are things we miss or don't notice about ourselves until they are exposed—until they are brought to light.

Pictures are designed to show the negative and the positive.

So, before you beat yourself up about the negatives of the picture let me tell you about the positives.

God wants us to focus on the snapshot of our true identity—our spirit housed in our form.

When we see that snapshot of our body and spirit aligned, the negatives will be developed into positives.

I know some of us came out of the darkroom too soon.

We were prematurely exposed to the light—not fully developed, still struggling with who we are, etc.

God created you.

He brought you into being.

He produced you in His image, in His likeness.

You are a duplicate, a reproduction of God Himself.

You were created in the image of God—male and female.

He created us.

He pulled out the male and the female from His Spirit.

God is God. He is multifaceted.

There are many sides to Him and many sides to us.

I want to expound upon the female part of God—woman.

When God wanted a helpmate (helpful partner) for Adam, He caused a deep sleep to fall upon him.

Genesis 2:22 states, "Then the rib which the LORD God had taken from man He made into a woman, and He brought her to the man."

One interesting thing about this scripture is the word *man*.

I asked God these questions.

"Why are you saying you took the rib from *man*?"

"Why are you saying you brought the woman to man?"

"Why are you not saying you brought the woman to Adam?"

I believe God shared some things with me concerning this.

What I am allowed to put in this book now is that God took the rib from man, and He made woman.

God fashioned woman and took her to man.

He styled her and custom made every inch of her.

(I will explain more about that in another book, wow!)

Notice God did not breathe into the woman.

He took a rib from man and created her.

"Wait a minute, God. Why did you breathe into the man and not the woman? Don't women deserve your breath, too?"

This is what I asked God when I realized He didn't breathe into the woman.

But, in my asking, God revealed to me that He really did breathe into the woman.

I, with my little religious self, could not see until God started to wrap my religion in His truth.

Where I was blind I could now see.

He showed me that the breath was already in the woman when He breathed into the man.

God didn't have to breathe again because the first time He exhaled His Spirit, His Ruwach kind of breath into man, *life* was given.

Anytime you're in the breath of God, you're in the Spirit of God.

Spirit is the Way.

Spirit is Truth.

Spirit is Life.

But, check this out.

Since truth doesn't stop there, everything that God is the man became.

As stated before man was formed.

God reached inside Himself, inside His breath, inside His Spirit, to bring man forth making him a living soul.

Then God reached inside of man who was originally inside of God to bring forth a helpful partner for man in the form of woman.

He didn't create her from dirt.

What are you saying, Cristi?

I'm saying it's time for truth to blast off in your life.

I already know what God is going to say next.

Everybody won't be able to handle it. But, I want you to know it's really ok.

I realize you cannot handle what you don't understand, and you don't understand what you can't handle.

Ask God to give you two graces right now.

(1) The grace to handle.

(2) The grace to understand.

God is multi-dimensional.

He is loving yet powerful, merciful yet a judge, all powerful and sovereign.

He has numerous sides that we've yet to discover. God is full of mysteries that only the Holy Spirit can reveal to us.

First Corinthians 2: 6-10 reads, "However, we speak

wisdom among those who are mature, yet not the wisdom of this age, nor of the rulers of this age, who are coming to nothing.

"But we speak the wisdom of God in a mystery, the hidden *wisdom* which God ordained before the ages for our glory, which none of the rulers of this age knew; for had they known, they would not have crucified the Lord of glory.

"But as it is written: 'Eye has not seen, nor ear heard, nor have entered into the heart of man the things which God has prepared for those who love Him.'

"But God has revealed them to us through His Spirit. For the Spirit searches all things, yes, the deep things of God."

Let's focus for a minute on verse nine.

Pray, asking God to open you to this truth.

"But as it is written: 'Eye has not seen, nor ear heard, nor have entered into the heart of man the things which God has prepared for those who love Him.'"

When God breathed Himself into man, He breathed everything Spirit.

He knew man would be placed on earth as a representation of Him.

So, God created man's form, and He breathed His Spirit into man causing him to become a living soul.

Man was in God's Spirit.

When God wanted a helpful partner for man, He created woman from the man's rib.

He did not have to breathe into her because the spirit of the woman already existed in man when God breathed into his nostrils making him a living soul.

Since she was alive inside of man, there was no reason for God to breathe again.

She simply breathed when he pulled her out of man's rib.

God breathed in to breathe out.

He basically pulled the woman out of man.

He pulled male and female out of Himself at the

same time.

He pulled the woman out of His Spirit to be a helpful partner to man. In His image He created them male and female.

Like Genesis 1:27 states, "So God created man in His own image; in the image of God, He created him; male and female He created them."

(My God, I so want to write some more stuff right here, but God says not now—whew!)

I want you to understand this fully. You existed way before you were formed and fashioned.

We're taught that life begins when the sperm attaches itself to an egg. But I beg to differ—that is the conception phase.

Life did not ever begin—life always was.

God is life.

Since He is life and has always existed, so have you because you are from Him.

You are an extension of God.

You are spirit. You don't need improving. You are from God. You are complete in your spirit.

Again, I urge you to get up, go slip into your spirit because that is the real you.

That is who you are.

So the next time you ponder the question, "Who am I? Remember that you are a spirit from God surrounded by your form, your body.

WHAT AM I?

Now, I would like to pose this question, "What are you?"

If our spirit is who we are, then what are we?

Ask yourself, "What am I?"

Listen carefully to your spirit because the answer lies on the inside of you.

When God spoke to my spirit about including "what we are" in this book, I thought, "Ok, God, this is not making sense to me."

Then He revealed to me what He is.

"What" defines the true nature of something—the sum of its characteristics.

What am I?

What I am includes my name.

What I am encompasses my purpose.

What I am contains is my breath.

What I am comprises my assignments.

What I am is my flavor.

When you discover what you are, you will express yourself instead of trying to impress others.

Your expression and communication, will flow from your spirit—the true you.

The impressions you've been signaling in your form—trying to amaze others—will cease.

The answer to what we are, resides inside of us, in our spirit, waiting to be unlocked, unleashed, and loosened.

When who you are, your spirit, is awakened, what you are begins to stir.

Your true identity, your spirit, reveals what you genuinely are.

In other words, your spirit identifies and reveals your expression, your purpose, your flavor.

The breath of God breathes an awakening in your spirit bringing life to every area of your being.

Your spirit breathes an awakening in what you are

which includes your purpose and the other things I mentioned above.

When God breathed the breath of His Spirit into the form of Adam, the Bible explains that Adam became a living soul.

When God's Spirit made contact with Adam's form, his earthly body—God's expression of Himself through Adam's spirit—began to awaken, move, shift, and stir Adam's form, every inch of him, inside and out, tangible and intangible.

The life of Adam's spirit was now manifested in his body, in his being—he was now a living soul.

See, Adam's form was transformed when God breathed into his nostrils.

Adam's spirit, his essence, connected with his form during this transaction.

Adam became a living soul propelling who and what he was into the earth's realm.

Well, Cristi, what do you mean?

Like Adam, our forms, our bodies, house our spirit—
who we are—and our spirit contains what we are.

The breath of God resulted in Adam becoming a
living soul. Adam came alive.

When God's spirit connected with Adams' form, he
was transformed.

Everything God breathed into Adam, his name and
the purpose for which he was created came to life.

Let me shift here for a minute.

Adam was not birthed from the womb of a woman.

He had no earthly parents to name him.

He was birthed from the womb of God—from God's
Spirit.

God named Adam.

Stay with me now.

I ask you this, "Why did God name Adam?"

Adam was called *man* for the longest.

So, why did God decide to name man Adam?

A name is a word or a combination of words by

which a person, place, thing, or thought is designated, called, or thought to be.

Names are significant.

They help establish you on earth.

Names are often attached to your purpose—your reason for being.

As parents, we have the task of naming our children. So, be very careful what you name your child because what you name someone is what they will answer to.

Adam means man. One formed from the ground.

God called man Adam to designate him on earth to correlate with his purpose.

Each of us has a purpose which oftentimes connects with the name we are given.

When God breathed his breath into man, man's purpose and reason to exist resided in God's breath.

When the man's form awakened and became alive, God named him Adam.

Then God commanded Adam's purpose, which came

along with particular assignments.

Sometimes we refer to our assignments as our calling.

So you see, when man was named, his purpose began to move.

When his purpose was apparent, he carried out the assignments associated with his purpose.

Church folks, we have it backwards.

Many of us are trying to perform our assignments without knowing who we are—spirit.

We try to perform our assignments without checking with our spirit to help us identify what we are which includes our purpose.

We walk around doing things, hit and miss, full of fear and anxiety because we are blind, confused, disillusioned, disoriented, etc.

We do this because we are assignment focused without knowing who we are and void of understanding what we are.

We have it backwards.

Remember, you have a form—your body—which houses who you are—your spirit.

You are given a name and purposed to perform your assignments.

Don't get it twisted.

Some of us are stuck in hearing the call—the assignments—without knowing our name and purpose, what we are, without knowing who we are.

We all have a kingdom purposed assignment to be manifested on earth.

What is your name?

What is your purpose?

What are your assignments associated with your purpose?

Do you know?

As previously state, your name, your purpose, and your assignments collectively define what you are. By knowing these things, it helps you more accurately answer the question posed earlier in this chapter, "What Am I?"

Man was formed from the earth, given the breath of life, his spirit, named and purposed to have dominion and authority on the earth.

Adam—named by God—was to call and to name, thus, the process continues, but I digress.

Genesis 2:19 reads, "Out of the ground the LORD God formed every beast of the field and every bird of the air, and brought them to Adam to see what he would call them. And whatever Adam called each living creature that was its name."

To me, this verse exemplifies assignments following purpose.

The first part of Genesis 2:20 states, "…Adam gave names to all cattle, to the birds of the air, and to every beast of the field…"

Again, this signifies Adam performing another purpose related assignment.

See, the man God named Adam was now naming things.

Whenever something is given a name, that's what it answers to helping to carry out the creation's purpose.

Whatever name Adam gave the cattle, birds, and beasts, contained their purpose and assisted them in carrying out their functions—their assignments.

Adam did not create the forms of the cattle, birds, and beasts. God did that.

Then, God purposed Adam with authority to name them.

The animals were formed but they had no names, no earthly purpose to answer to and perform their assignments until Adam acted in his purpose of creative authority to perform one of his assignments of naming them.

The horse didn't have a neigh until Adam named it.

When Adam named the horse, the horse's purpose

was manifested as well as the various assignments the horse would perform—one being the horse's neigh.

Everything about the horse began to function—glory to God.

Dolphins didn't behave as dolphins until Adam named them.

Cats couldn't meow until Adam named them.

The cat responded to its name by functioning.

Do you see the pattern?

Everything Adam named—designated it to be— functioned in its purpose and performed its assignments.

When the named connects with its purpose get ready for the assignments to be manifested.

The named is purposed to perform its given assignments for all to see.

The bible explicitly states that *you* were created.

Look at God.

You were created—past tense.

You were created in God's image, in His likeness.

God had already produced you in eternity past so He could reproduce you on earth.

As He reproduced you on earth, He replicated Himself through you for a precise purpose with specific assignments—what you are—which resides inside your spirit.

When God breathed the breath of his Spirit into man, the breath of God, the Spirit of God, not only included who man was, but it also contained what man was.

Like man—Adam—you are a spirit in a form—your body—dwelling on earth full of purpose and designated assignments to follow.

The earth is waiting on you.

I've heard it preached and have said it myself, that destiny is waiting on me, or that we were created for destiny.

However, this time God said, *"I am reversing your way of thinking when it comes to destiny and purpose.*

"You were formed for destiny, but you were created for a purpose."

Destiny means an event or course of events that will inevitably happen in the future—a predetermined line of events expected and bound to happen.

Purpose means an anticipated outcome intended or something that guides your planned actions.

Back in Eternity Past, God, already knowing who my earthly parents would be, breathed the breath of His Spirit upon my mother's womb exhaling my established destiny—the predetermined line of events expected and bound to happen in my life.

When God was ready to see Himself in the form of me, when He was ready to see an expression of Himself in which only I could accomplish, when He was ready for me to be born, guess what He did?

He pulled me out of His Spirit, breathed upon my mother's womb and placed me inside of her.

On July 27, 1965, the predetermined Cristi was born.

The course of my earthly life began so that I could fulfill my purpose—the anticipated outcome that guided the planned actions for my life.

Who I am and what I am arrived with me at the time I was born.

My mother named me Cristi Renea to distinguish what I was to be called on earth.

Although Cristi is my name, Cristi is not who I am.

I am spirit.

See, God doesn't operate like humans.

God creates our form.

He gives us life—His Spirit.

He places our purpose inside of us.

He equips us with the knowledge, skills, and ability to allow our purpose to flow through the assignments associated with our purpose.

That's why it's essential that you know who you are, spirit, and to hear what you are from your spirit residing within you—therein inhabits your purpose with assignments to follow.

Let me give you a biblical analogy from Genesis 1:3, "Then God said, 'Let there be light'; and there was light."

Sounds like God's creative thought moved to His mouth, and He spoke light into existence. This is an example demonstrating a part of what God is—a Creator.

Let's break it down.

When God's creative thought about light transferred to His spoken word about light coming into existence, light appeared.

Where did the light come from?

The light came from God.

He is light.

He called light from Himself.

When He called light forth, light answered by appearing.

Same with us, we were in God's creative thoughts.

The verse also states that, "···God saw the light, that it was good..."

Why was the light good?

Because God is good and everything about Him is good—including you.

You can't even spell the word "good" without including God.

Another reason God saw the light was good is because light was now operating and functioning in its purpose carrying out its assignments—what it is.

Light already existed when God called it forth.

Light was manifested on earth because it was destined to be here.

When light began to operate and function in its created purpose, its intended outcome, what light was called to do was now in full effect.

I like to say that light was operating in its breath.

So, when God said let there be *(insert your name)*, you came into existence as an extension of Him.

I ask you again, what are you?

What is your purpose?

What is your breath?

Your name distinguishes you on the earth—it's what you answer to.

Your purpose aligned with its assignments, helps identify what you are.

How can you answer to a name filled with your purpose and the assignments associated with it if you really don't know who you are, spirit?

When you don't know what you've been purposed to do, you'll answer to a barrage of names that don't fit you.

Oh, come on now. You know what I'm referring to.

You'll answer to Mistress.

You'll answer to Shame.

You'll answer to Homosexuality.

You'll answer to Low Self-Esteem.

You'll answer to Crack-Addict.

You'll answer to Guilt.

You'll answer to Pride.

You'll answer to Death.

You'll answer to anything.

The problem is we've been answering to names and things other people have given us instead of answering to what God calls us.

Therefore, we now have an identity crisis simply because we do not know who.

We don't know what we are—our purpose and the assignments that go along with it.

What are you?

What is your purpose?

What were you created to be and do?

What part of God did He place in you to be manifested on earth?

You are uniquely created to do things only *you* can do.

No one can do these things for you.

People can imitate you and even try to duplicate what you do, but the original gift (purpose, breath, assignment) resides in *you*.

If your breath is to teacher, then teach—traditionally or non-traditionally.

Teach where you are.

Although millions of teachers exist, there is a specific breath to your teaching that no one else has.

You have a sphere of influence that only you are intended to teach in.

If your breath is to design, then, baby design.

Marc Jacobs, Antonio Melani, Badgley Mischka or no other designer can design like you.

Cristi, those people are well known designers.

Guess what?

So are you.

You are well known to the One, who placed the gift inside of you in the first place.

The difference between those designers and you is

they know what they are.

They responded to their purpose carrying out the attached assignments.

They decided to operate in their breath, in their gift, in their purpose.

They connected with what they are and walked in it—creating an original designer-line every time.

The most influential talk show host of all time didn't get to be what she is simply by chance.

No.

She is what she is because she heard her purpose, "talk show host", resonating within her.

She responded to the predetermined gift (purpose) within her—the breath of a talk show host.

Then she breathed that specific breath and the assignments associated with her purpose bringing life to her as well as to others.

The bible states that your gifts will make room for you.

Your gifts have life and breath.

When you begin to answer, operate, and function in what you are, then you will see your purpose in action.

You will begin to live more fully and breathe life into others.

Your predetermined-self will meet and kiss.

Your purpose will go with you—transforming you and those you come in contact with.

That's when God will bend over the balcony of heaven, look at you—the extended part of Him in you—and say, "It is good."

If you already know your purpose, then answer it— get moving.

If you don't know your purpose yet, shhh, be quiet.

Listen for it.

When you hear God call out to you, in your spirit, just say to Him, "Speak Lord."

He will reveal what you are to you.

Listen and keep listening.

While you are waiting to hear your purpose—what you are—give the devil back his fake I.D.

Erase from your mind those counterfeit names and actions that have been attached to you.

Go ahead and start praising God that your identity crisis is over.

Identity theft has been resolved.

The Holy Ghost is issuing you a *new* Identity Card stamped with your name and purpose defining what you are—glory to God.

Remember, your purpose and the assignments associated with it collectively define what you are.

Many times the name given to you contains your purpose and assignments.

But, listen to your spirit, the real you, for full clarity in knowing what you are.

<u>Pray this prayer:</u>

Father God, I thank and praise you for my identity being established in you. I thank you that every misconception of my identity has been replaced with Truth. Today, I accept what I am as defined by you. I call forth my purpose to align with my spirit—the REAL me. I ask that the true manifestation of my purpose—what I am—be revealed, in Jesus' name, Amen.

WHY AM I HERE?

It may seem like I am repeating myself in this book.

That is intentional since every part connects leading back to the title, *Free to Be···Me.*

Every part of the book relates to your true identity, your spirit.

It's imperative that you grasp who you are and to embrace what you are to give you a better understanding of why you are here—it all ties in with your spirit.

Until you come full circle seeing yourself as a spirit housed in a body, you will constantly search for yourself—seeking your identity outwardly.

The fact of the matter is you were created to look inside yourself more than search for your identity outwardly.

All my life, I have been looking for me.

I've been trying to find me, trying to find myself,

trying to fulfill my purpose, trying to be what others wanted me to be, trying to live up to folks' expectations.

In my 44 years of trying, my life had been miserable.

Yes, you read correctly—forty-four years of trying to please and appease people, including my family—trying to measure-up to their perception of me.

I know I am loved by my family.

But, am I understood by them?

My answer would be no.

This lack of being misunderstood sometimes places me in a most awkward and uncomfortable position.

Is it ok that some of them do not understand me?

Of course it is very acceptable.

It really does not matter who understands me or not as long as I understand myself.

Understanding who I am, I understand what I am, and why I exist.

In understanding these things, I understand me—the

real me, my spirit.

In discussing who and what we are, I shared that we are all born with a predetermined plan.

We all have a purpose.

We have heard destiny and purpose preached in pulpits all over the country.

Although it is good that we be knowledgeable about destiny and purpose, a huge part of what we are, we also need to have more understanding with this knowledge.

We, in the body of Christ, have flipped over pews and shouted down aisles because we are told that we have a destiny and a purpose assigned to us.

While that is ok, we fail to realize there is something standing between our destiny and our purpose.

The missing link is the process.

Process is like a dirty word because it involves waiting.

We are instantaneous people.

We do not like waiting for anything.

Process also includes some things like being misunderstood, rejected, and cast out.

Being processed for your purpose costs you.

Process is a continuous action, operation, and series of changes taking place in a definite manner for a specific purpose.

Process involves molding, shaping, forming, sculpting.

This process I'm mentioning is called "everyday living".

What continuous series of changes are you going through?

When in your holding cells—waiting periods—what weights are you carrying?

What weights are crushing you, molding you, shaping you, forming you, sculpting you and preparing you for your purpose?

Are you still shouting about your purpose now?

Can you handle the weight in your wait?

Mind you, during the process, your purpose is often carried out simultaneously.

The processing does not occur in a straight line of time—not the way we define time.

The purpose for your life is enormous—the greater the purpose, the greater the process.

Can you handle it?

Your purpose is not just about you.

It is a kingdom assignment for you to share with other folks assigned to your life as well.

Previously, I discussed the breath of God.

Well, you have people assigned to you who you need to breathe on to give them life.

They are waiting on you to get into your position of knowing who you really are.

So, there is no time for you to curl up and die—though you may feel like it sometimes.

When being processed, this is not the time for you to

quit or throw your hands up and walk away.

If you do, the people assigned to you will not be able to breathe either.

Believe it or not there are people breathing on you right now, giving you life.

Feel my breath on you now as read this book.

We are all in this thing together.

Purpose is not a game.

Purpose is a gift.

Your gift does not belong to you alone. It is for others, too.

God entrusted you with the gift of purpose for you to complete your assignments associated with it.

The process of your purpose links to why you are here.

As stated, when going through the process, you are carrying out your purpose.

Believe it or not, the process began the day you were born.

Although parts of the process are hard at times, it is essential that you make it.

You cannot faint.

Please do not give up.

Oh, I know we do faint at times.

We frequently quit because it becomes tiresome and hard.

Being shaped and formed does not always feel good.

If we equate our process with clay, the similarities are astounding.

When you want to change what you have formed with clay, you smash it, reshape it, and remold it all over again.

Like clay on the potter's wheel, the process of our purpose is continuously being fashioned by the Potter.

We are marred, broken here, and cracked there so we will not be leaky vessels.

God reshapes and remolds us to contain and hold what He has placed inside of us.

Living (the process) consists of joys, sorrows, pains, happiness, pits, palaces, mountains, valleys, etc.

Living is all part of the molding, crushing, shaping, forming, and sculpting of our purpose.

Here is a partial list of life events that help in the purpose process: alcoholism, over or under eating, drugs, education, fornicating, marriage, pride, loving yourself, gossip, maturing, dating, homosexuality, loving others, spouses walking out, raising children, being childless, loneliness, quiet times, rejection, friendships, ridicule, accolades, divorce, accomplishments, family, relationships, molestation, caring, suicide attempts, discipline, rape, recovery, recessions, promotions, raises, unemployment, hitting the jackpot, starting a business, moving, changing times, being single, etc.

All the daily things we go through are part of the process helping us to carry out our purpose— displaying why we are here.

These things can be categorized as weights or waits brought on by the natural course of living, God, you, Satan, or others.

Romans 8:28 reads, "···we know that all things work together for good to those who love God, to those who are the called according to His purpose."

Just because you've had some damage done to you, does not mean you are damaged goods—quite the contrary.

God loves you.

He takes your messes, mistakes, feeble attempts, mishaps and still joyously uses you for His glory.

You are here at this present time because God ordained you to be.

You could have been born earlier or later.

However, you are here now, in this appointed time for your specific purpose—for such a time as this.

Destiny and purpose play a pivotal role in why we are here.

Realize that Satan—an enemy of our soul—hates us, especially in our predetermined state.

The enemies of who we really are—spirit—want to kill us. This is one of the main reasons abortions exists.

The enemies, of who you are, want to kill you before you begin—want to kill God's predetermined state for you.

When God communicates with your spirit, calling you a Business Owner, Teacher, Author, Preacher, Designer, etc., the enemy whispers acidic lies in your ears saying, "God didn't tell you that. You can't do this. Who and what do you think you are? You are nobody."

Before long, we begin to believe these lies.

Our actions follow what our ears have listened to for so long.

We tuck far away the predetermined plan that God placed in us completely forgetting about it.

We abort our dreams, our visions, and our purpose. Then we walk around empty and void because the purpose for which we were created eludes us.

We no longer believe in ourselves or God.

We believe the lies that we are unworthy of producing anything good.

Our purpose seems unattainable because we see streets and highways lined with detour signs and road blocks sprinkled along the way.

We drive on thinking these detours and road blocks are part of our fated demise.

I call you to remember the process that brings our purpose to fruition has detours and road blocks, but our purpose is still alive.

Again, remember what Romans 8:28 reminds us, "···we know that all things work together for good to those who love God, to those who are the called according to His purpose."

So, even in the midst of wrong turns, speed bumps, and missed shifts, the road to purpose is still awaiting us.

We might have to backup, make U-turns, or shift gears.

However, we can find ourselves right back on the highway of our process to purpose.

Can I tell you something?

These mishaps are ok because ultimately your purpose outweighs the process.

The process is to purify, refine, and redefine us for our purpose so it can flourish throughout the earth.

I know the heat becomes intense.

The distractions seem very tempting and tantalizing.

The pain is often great.

It has to be, at times, because you were created for God's glory, created so the awesomeness He placed in you can shine through.

As your purpose is displayed, it is God—His breath in you—that others are seeing in you.

Remember, who you are—spirit.

Your spirit is God inside of you.

Keep in mind, when God breathed into Adam's nostrils, he became a living soul.

You are a living soul—an expression of God.

Your conforming to His image is merely you tapping into who you are—the spirit of God residing inside of you.

Sometimes God has to burn some stuff off of and out of you.

He examines you for hindrances that interfere with your purpose and break those things off so you represent Him precisely here on earth.

I want to encourage you.

You have the stamina to endure.

While you are in your waiting room, wait.

Isaiah 40:31 communicates, "But those who wait on the LORD shall renew their strength; they shall mount up with wings like eagles, they shall run and not be weary, they shall walk and not faint."

While waiting on God, you trust Him to bring to pass

the purpose He placed inside of you.

Your life is not over.

God has not given up on you.

Please stop giving up on yourself.

Pick yourself up.

Dust yourself off and continue waiting on Him even more.

Stop buckling under the weight while waiting.

Sometimes we pace back and forth in our waiting rooms stunned by circumstances and situations that have left us in a comatose state.

We cry to get out.

We try to step into our purpose instead of allowing the process to release our purpose day-by-day.

The only way your purpose releases out of you is on the wings of the process.

Remember, process establishes you.

We become so anxious to perform the assignments associated with our purpose that we step out before we are mature enough to handle the weight of our purpose.

Purpose is not free. It costs a lot.

Think about Jesus.

It cost Him his life to fulfill His ultimate purpose, to fulfill His kingdom assignments, to fulfill why He was here.

His purpose was not all about Him.

It was about God's plan, you, me, and the world.

I state again, purpose is costly.

Are you willing to pay the price to fulfill your purpose?

It is going to cost you.

It may cost you your family.

Are you willing?

It may cost you your friends.

It may cost you some getting up early and some staying up late at night.

It may cost you your reputation and eating some

humble pie.

Are you willing?

It may cost you being talked about, labeled or branded crazy.

It will cost you a dying to safe and familiar ways of doing things, dying to how others want you to behave, dying to the status quo.

Are you willing?

Let's transition.

Are you constantly wondering why you are merely existing and not living?

Why you are so unhappy?

Why you are never satisfied?

Could it be that you have yet to tap into your true-self releasing the gifts of your purpose God placed within you?

I ask you again:

What is your purpose?

What are you designed for?

What is your breath?

What is your passion?"

When you listen to your spirit to find the answers to these questions, the answer to why you are here becomes more evident.

It's just waiting to burst forth.

Your arrival on earth was a divine manifestation of God.

You are destined to be here at this moment, in this time, for such a time as this.

You are essential to the kingdom.

Your breath—what you are, which flows from your spirit, who you are—is needed to breathe life upon the earth in a manner that only you can do.

The next time you wonder, "Why am I here?"

Know that the breath in you, which contains your purpose, is needed on the earth at this very moment, in this time, for such a time as this.

Now That I Know

Knowing who you are, what you are, and why you exist conveys that you are filled with great purpose and a sense of hope—that you are valuable and worthy.

Earlier, I shared that purpose is sometimes painful and costly.

Have the costs and pains of hardships caused you to develop a welded womb?

Cristi, what is a welded womb?

I am so glad you asked.

In 1 Samuel 1:1-7, we read the story of Elkanah who had two wives, Hannah and Penninah. Penninah bore Elkanah children. Hannah did not.

First Samuel 1:3-7 goes as follows, "This man [Elkanah] went up from his city yearly to worship and sacrifice to the Lord of hosts in Shiloh.

"Also the two sons of Eli, Hophni and Phinehas, the

priests of the Lord, were there.

"And whenever the time came for Elkanah to make an offering, he would give portions [of the meat] to Peninnah his wife and to all her sons and daughters.

"But to Hannah he would give a double portion [of the meat], for he loved Hannah, although the Lord had closed her womb.

"And her [Hannah's] rival [Penninah] also provoked her severely, to make her miserable, because the Lord had closed her womb.

"So it was, year by year, when she [Penninah] went up to the house of the Lord, that she provoked her [Hannah]; therefore she [Hannah] wept and did not eat."

We see here that Elkanah gave a double portion to Hannah to compensate her for her lack of children and to demonstrate his love for her.

He loved Hannah even though the Lord had closed her womb.

Her womb was what I call a *welded womb.*

All women have a womb—uterus, if you will.

The womb is the place where conception takes place.

It is the place where things are formed or produced.

The word *produce* means to bring into existence, to create, to bring forth, to give birth.

The Bible states that the Lord had closed Hannah's womb.

Now, you know that something closed prevents the passage of anything entering or exiting.

Nothing goes in and nothing comes out.

Hannah's womb was welded.

It was closed.

It was shut.

Although Hannah had sex with her husband, knew him intimately, and received the seeds he deposited into her, she was still unable to produce offspring.

Men are releasers.

Women are receivers.

Women are vessels that collect and contain.

When women are intimate with their husbands, have casual sex, or just sex it up with someone else's man, there is a moment when the man releases his seed.

The woman receives the man's seed.

A deposit is made.

If it is her time of ovulating, we know that one, two, three, or more of his seeds—sperm—can attach itself to the woman's egg. Thus, conception occurs. The woman becomes pregnant.

Just as it is in the natural, so it is in the spiritual realm.

When we trust Jesus as our Savior and Lord, we become intimate with Him.

We listen to His sweet words.

We grow more and more curious about Him— wanting to know every detail.

We become secure in knowing the depth of His love for us.

We open up and start loving Him, spending long hours at a time with Him.

Our intimacy together grows rapidly.

We trust Him completely, believing every word about who He is, what He is, and why He exists.

Suddenly, all our defenses drop.

He asks if we believe the truth about Him.

We say, "Yes."

We are so intertwined that He begins to release His Spirit into our spiritual womb.

He deposits more of Himself into us.

He impregnates us giving us more of His spiritual life, so we are able to fulfill our divine purpose, fully becoming who we are, what we are, and going through the process of knowing, releasing, and experiencing why we are here.

Well, that seems like a beautiful thing, and it is. Wouldn't you agree?

But, we have a problem, people.

I ask you this.

Where are our spiritual babies—the results of our purpose?

In the natural, pregnancy is usually a nine month process.

However, most of us—especially us church folks—have been pregnant with our purpose for 10, 20, or 30 years having yet to see the baby.

We walk around saying, "Girl, God is about to do something in me. That message pastor preached made my baby leap."

We shout, fall out, have hands laid on us, run from one conference and prophet to another trying to get a word. "I need a word. I just need a word."

When really we don't need "a" word, we need THE WORD.

John 1:1 states, "In the beginning was the Word, and the Word was with God, and the Word was God."

If you look at this verse of scripture, you'll see that

the *W* is capitalized because John is referring to the Lord, who is THE WORD—THE WORD that we need.

One word from God can change our life forever.

I believe God shared with me why He is THE WORD.

"The" legitimizes a thing—it represents only one, meaning there is none other.

God shared with me, *"If I had said I am "a" word, it would have been illegitimate because "a" indicates another exists.*

"I am not "a" Word.

"I am THE WORD.

"I am not "a" god,

I am THE only true and living God—besides me, there is no other."

He also said, *"Ask them are they having MY babies or are they having bastards?*

"Are their purposes legitimate or illegitimate?

"Did THE WORD impregnate them with a purpose or was it 'a' word because many of their babies do not

resemble me?"

If your purpose is all about you, then you've been sleeping with the enemy.

If your ministry is all about glorifying yourself or how well you make the people shout, then you've been fooling around with the enemy.

If your purpose is all puffed up in pride and wrapped up in impressing folks, then you've been creeping with the enemy.

If your purpose has some children resembling jealousy, envy, greed, backbiting, or gossip, you've been intimate with the enemy instead of being intimate with God.

God is not obligated to take care of anything that is not of Him.

Babies have their father's features as well as their mother's.

Who does your baby look like?

Look closely at your baby named Purpose.

Does your baby (Purpose) look like God or the enemy?

Who yo' baby daddy?

Be careful. Welded wombs can be shut by you as well as by the enemy.

The bible informs us that Hannah had an adversary that provoked her severely to make her miserable because the Lord had closed her womb.

Hannah's adversary, her opponent, her foe, her hostile enemy, the other woman, Penninah, provoked, teased, and ridiculed Hannah because she was barren—had a welded womb.

Penninah can represent a demonic spirit, a decoy, sent by the enemy to distract, devour, and destroy you and your purpose by getting you to abort your promise, abort your seed, and abort your purpose.

I am sent by God to tell you, in this book, that the devil is a liar.

Your baby will not die but live.

You will not abort.

Your baby is not only about you. It is a kingdom child.

This baby must be manifested on earth because lives are depending on it.

Stop telling everybody you're pregnant.

Everyone can't handle you expecting.

Some folks aren't happy that you have life on the inside of you.

Various people will not believe that you're pregnant with a purpose.

You know how it is in the natural.

When you first find out you're pregnant, you tell somebody.

They say, "You lying. You don't look like it. You are not even showing. Are you sure?"

When you discover you are spiritually pregnant with a purpose, you are so excited and want to share it with everybody—just like in the natural.

They may say, "Girl, are you sure God called you into the ministry?"

"Are you sure you're supposed to be a business owner?"

"Did God really tell you to write a book?"

Penninah spirits are negative naysayers—constant sources of discouragement.

If you're not careful, they will cause you to have a miscarriage.

God gave your purpose—your baby—to you, not to anyone else.

Penninah is not suppose to see what's going on or even understand it.

That's why it's your baby and not hers.

Hannah was not only barren in her womb but the constant ridicule from Penninah caused barrenness in her mind.

How many of you have been or are currently barren in your mind?

Being barren in your mind puts you in a state of hopelessness.

Have you been there?

Are you in a hopeless state of mind right now feeling like all hell is coming against you—not knowing which way to turn?

Alone, at your wits end, not knowing what to do?

I assure you that you are not alone.

I've been in this isolated place. So have others.

Hannah was there.

In 1 Samuel 1:8-18, the bible conveys Hannah's actions.

She wept.

She couldn't eat.

Her soul was bitter.

She prayed to the Lord.

She cried in anguish allowing her situation to get the best of her.

She let the Penninah spirit creep in bringing her

down with depression.

Even in her pain, in the midst of her torment, Hannah prayed to the Lord.

It was pain that pushed Hannah into prayer, into worship, into a place of intimacy with God.

She did not have anyone who could change her situation but God.

Hannah was experiencing the process of her purpose.

Since her womb was welded, she knew if there was any chance of becoming pregnant—coming out of this barren state in her life—she had to position herself in a place of intimacy with God for the gestation of her purpose to produce a healthy deliverance.

Frequently, painful situations, trials, tests, etc. cause us to pull away, retreating from God.

When we draw back from Him, we often find ourselves misaligned in our relationship with Him.

We seek more to have our horizontal relationships

with people in tack rather than seeking to have our vertical relationship with God in alignment.

Misalignment with God is like your car being out of kilter.

When driving, the car has a tendency to veer to the right or left instead of staying in the center, on course.

If you're not careful, that misalignment can cause you to have a blowout and wreck.

I believe many of us in the body of Christ suffer from blowouts and wrecks.

We are running into ditches and off of curbs because we are veering off course.

We are not staying centered.

We are misaligned.

We are out of position—wrecking spiritually.

I want to encourage you.

It is never too late for you to be realigned, repositioned.

Repositioning involves an inevitable change.

It involves you being moved from your current state to another.

Hannah had to be repositioned—not just physically, but, emotionally, and spiritually.

Her way of thinking had to be altered for change to occur.

Can you deal with being repositioned for necessary changes to occur so you can experience being who you are, what you are, and living out why you exist, which places you in your position of purpose?

Repositioning causes you to shift, move, change places, and rarely is it a onetime occurrence. It's ongoing, continuous.

When God repositions us, it's constant updating if you will.

We continuously use old versions of software in our mindsets, prayer life, worship, praise, and love for God.

Out of love and our willingness, He downloads the most current version of software to shift, move, and change us from a stationary position to an active and current one.

It's like me repositioning my furniture.

I have gotten accustomed to where it is, and it's not doing anything for me anymore. So, I decide to rearrange it.

In order to get my furniture placed in a new location, I grab hold of it and pick it up.

If it's too heavy, I tug and pull it. I shift it, move it, twist it, and lift it until I have it in my desired location.

It's the same with God.

He wants to move us from negative mindsets to renewed ways of thinking, from the outward into our spirit, from religion to an intimate relationship with Him.

Like bulky hard to move furniture, we are hard to reposition. We want to remain stationary.

Unlike furniture which has no voice, we do.

We can communicate with God.

We can give Him a "Yes Lord" and let the repositioning occur.

Instead, many times, we choose to remain silent in our fixed ways.

God has to grab us, pick us up, pull us, lift us, and shift us to other locations to level us for our purposeful change to occur.

This repositioning—grabbing, pulling, lifting and shifting—may cause pain and discomfort.

Change can be that way.

You may be too heavy and weighty.

You may get tired and need a second wind.

But, if you trust that God knows exactly where you need to be, where you need to be repositioned, you can best believe your placement will be effective and efficient.

My sofas are really big, but I frequently move them around.

Sometimes I ask my husband, Greg, to help me, or I

drag them myself.

It may seem easier with Greg's help but that's usually just not the case.

Why?

He doesn't know the exact spot I want to place the furniture.

Yes, I tell him.

But, just because I tell him, doesn't mean he catches my vision for the room's layout.

Anyone can have sight. But, do you have a vision?

Sight gives you the ability to recognize something with your eyes. You only see the possibilities.

Vision allows you to look beyond the possibilities into the impossible.

Vision is the act or power of anticipating that which will or may come to be.

When rearranging my furniture, I've already envisioned the end result of what I want.

I've caught the vision of the sofas, chairs, etc. being

repositioned in their soon-to-be spots.

So, when others can't grasp your vision, they might tell you that it will not work, or it can't possibly happen.

People will tell you God is not repositioning you to move you to a new job.

God is not shifting you from an employee to an employer.

God is not pulling you out of prostitution to be a preacher.

They just notice your current state because they haven't caught the vision.

They see where you are and not where you will end up.

Where you are currently is not your end.

You will end right where you started—spirit.

There hasn't been a time I've rearranged our furniture or remodeled our home and my husband has not loved it.

As a matter of fact, when he looks at the end result, he says, "Baby, I see it now!"

That's because he sees the manifested vision I had for the room.

Let me tell you, there is a big difference between sight and vision.

What do you see?

What are you looking at?

Do you have sight?

Or do you have vision?

Does your vision of yourself allow you to catch a glimpse beyond your present state to be aware of who you are, what you are, and why you are here?

Does your vision of yourself go beyond what you currently see?

Your possibilities are endless and within reach.

There is no need for them to be in your range of sight—just catch a vision of them.

The vision of your possibilities comes first.

Then they manifest into sight for you and others to see.

Why?

Nothing is impossible for you because you are spirit.

Separate the word impossible.

You have im + possible.

I call it, I'm Possible.

I'm Possible to do all things through Christ, who strengthens me.

I'm Possible is who, what, and why I am—deep inside.

Your new catchphrase can now be, *Mission: I'm Possible.*

Allow the word impossible to be transformed in your mind and being.

Change your thinking to "I'm Possible".

Matthew 17: 18-20 states, "And Jesus rebuked the demon, and it came out of him; and the child was cured from that very hour.

"Then the disciples came to Jesus privately and said, 'Why could we not cast it out?'

"So Jesus said to them,

'Because of your unbelief; for assuredly,

"I say to you, if you have faith as a mustard seed, you will say to this mountain, 'Move from here to there,' and it will move; and nothing will be impossible for you."

Jesus tells us to have faith.

If our faith is the size of a mustard seed, it has so much power.

It has the ability to move mountains—glory to God.

You can stop looking at other people wishing you had faith like theirs.

We all have a certain measure of faith that carries weight and power—power that causes mountains to crumble and fall.

Your faith has the ability and strength to do things to cause extraordinary changes.

Faith has the power to move anything.

When true faith is activated in your spirit, things begin to move.

Even if that faith is small, when applied to mountains, they must still crumble and fall.

What mountains are hemming you in?

What mountains are blocking your purpose and its process?

What mountains are you trying to climb?

Do you want to know why you are so unsuccessful in your attempt to climb and go around your mountains?

It's because God did not tell you to go around or climb the mountains.

Yes, we sing songs to the contrary.

God said speak to the mountain.

By talking to the mountain, with your faith activated, the mountain moves.

It crumbles.

You have the faith to tell your mountain of lack, "Be

gone!"

You have the power to say to the mountain of depression, "Crumble and fall!"

You have the power to tell the mountain of adultery, "Move!"

Your existence can cause mountains to tremble.

You are just that powerful.

Yes I said the "P" word.

You are POWERFUL.

You are effective, potent, capable, influential, and strong.

You are POWERFUL.

Despite what you feel, regardless of where you are presently in your life.

You—the real you, your spirit—are "all that" and so much more.

We frequently allow enemies of our true being as well as our own voice to silence our spirit by telling us crippling defeating thoughts about ourselves.

Repeatedly, we hear that we are weak, feeble, frail and fragile—that things are impossible for us to accomplish.

These messages render us powerless.

Guess what?

The enemies of our true essence want us to see ourselves infirmed and broken.

If you remain in a powerless state, you will remain imprisoned to the lies thus denying who you are, what you are, and why you are here.

Remember, you have a purpose.

With your purpose, there is a process empowering you to be victorious, producing great works for God's kingdom here on earth.

When enemy tactics, like divorce, molestation, rape, or homosexuality are used to silence who, what, and why you are, exercise your faith within you to combat the sting.

Keep thinking, "I'm Possible."

Those enemy tactics and assaults are designed to silence your gloriousness, the real you,

But, these things are also part of your process to bring your purpose to the surface.

Sometimes the weight of your process can weaken you from becoming fully aware of your awesomeness—of the gloriously divine creation you are.

Abandonment is another obstacle in your purpose process that causes you to shy away from letting who, what, and why you are to radiate.

Adultery can place labels like weak and ineffective on you putting a stop to who and what you are as well as why you exist.

I encourage you to GET UP.

If you are victimized by low self-esteem causing you to display behaviors like frailty, feebleness, and unfruitfulness remember you are a spirit with a purpose designed to breathe your breath of life into others around you producing magnificent things in the world.

The enemies of our spirit use any means necessary to keep us from knowing who we are, what we are, and why we exist in Christ Jesus.

"For in Him [Christ] we live and move and have our being, as also some of your own poets have said, 'For we are also His offspring,'" Acts 17:28.

Wrong thinking paralyzes you and allows the power that God placed in you to become fruitless.

Paralysis halts your movement and actions. Immobility takes over.

We've allowed the enemies of our soul—fear, self-doubt, and other devices—to paralyze us by keeping us in a motionless state.

God created your spirit to be free not rigid and bound.

If we are created for freedom, why are we so restricted?

Why have we allowed ourselves to become entangled and ensnared in webs—tied up, enslaved?

Our superman and superwoman cloak of power has malfunctioned.

We are entrapped within by religion, other voices, and opinions with no way of escape.

We operate in the hero façade instead of being the real powerhouses we are.

We are chained by reflections of our own devices instead of being free people in the image of Christ.

Restriction and restraint prevent our freedom.

We are unshackled and emancipated.

We are free.

The word itself just sounds so liberating.

Inmates desire freedom.

Children can't wait to be liberated from their parents.

Caged animals long to roam unencumbered.

Babies housed in their mother's wombs restlessly await their time to be released.

We are all in pursuit of freedom—always chasing yet never attaining.

Why?

We were not created to chase and pursue ourselves.

What am I saying?

I am saying freedom is not what we do.

Freedom is who we are—we are free spirits.

When God breathed His breath into Adam, He breathed his Ruwach, His Neshamah, His Spirit, and His Life into him.

Adam was alive before He was formed.

He came from God in the first place.

When God wanted a representative and an ambassador of Himself on earth, He produced Adam thus the rest of the human race.

We are God's spirit encased in human bodies— human forms.

Please come to realize that your true essence, your true being is in your spirit.

God spoke this to my spirit, *"I am spirit—no one can capture spirit.*

"I am life—no one can chain life.

"I am breath—no one can shackle breath.

"No one can restrain, restrict, or bind me—for I am God.

"You are a part of me—the real you, your spirit.

"You are spirit and you are free."

We were created to be free. And we make the choice to live out our freedom in any manner we please.

We can choose to be bound, soar into being all that is inherently good within us, or whatever.

We make the choice.

We can choose to allow the enemy of our soul, people, labels, circumstances, situations, our present state of mind, our past, etc. to restrict and restrain us.

If we do this, we are not living out a God-kind-of-freedom which is full of life.

How does living effectively in freedom look?

While the Emancipation Proclamation was wonderful and brought freedom to slaves in the United States during the 1800's, here we are in the 21st century still enslaved.

Am I just referring to African Americans?

No, I am speaking to everyone.

Collectively, we are an enslaved society.

Slaves bound to someone, dominated by some influence, purchased, controlled, and owned by something.

Are you a slave?

Before you answer *no* so quickly, think of where you are right now.

Look beyond your physically state. Look at your mental and spiritual state as well.

Are you free in your mind?

Are you free in your thinking?

Are you free in your perceptions?

If you do not have a renewed mind or the mind of

Christ, then you are in bondage in your thoughts— enslaved and not free.

If your mind is in bondage, your thinking lacks freedom.

If there is no freedom in your thinking, your speech is guarded.

If your speech is guarded, your actions are limited.

Since your actions are limited, your life is imprisoned.

You are not free.

You are bound.

You are enslaved to a demonic, hostile system— trapped in slavery to not only the enemy but to yourself.

I ask again, "Are you free?"

Society demands that we look a certain way and dictates what is fashionable or not.

Nebulous groups define what's normal or not normal for us to do.

They tell us we have not arrived until we have a certain amount of money or live in the most upscale elaborate neighborhoods.

We hear repeated messages that we're to drive a certain type of car to be important—all kinds of controlling messages that enslave us—taskmasters, insisting we must purchase this, should have that, need the latest "what-have-you", should be first, must hurry before it's all gone, need this type of relationship, ought to have sex, now. The list goes on and on—enslavement, I tell you.

It's alright to take cues from these messages as long as they line up with who *you* are, what *you* are, and why *you* are here.

Check your spirit to know which messages will help you freely carry out your purpose.

We are even enslaved people in the church—bound by religion, traditions, preachers, pastors, programs, folks, etc.—slaves.

Do any of the following judgmental tradition-driven thoughts haunt you?

"The pastor said I have to attend church."

"The program won't go on if I am not there."

"I really don't want to go to church today, but, if I miss, they are going to look at me funny."

"We've always served communion on first and third Sundays."

"We don't pray like that."

"We stand for the reading."

"We sit for the reading."

If any of these thoughts, actions, or similar ones plagues you, then I want to let you know that you are being taunted by a slave-taskmaster mentality—unable to exercise your own freedom.

We are behaving as enslaved people instead of people created to be free.

We don't exercise our freedom because we allow ourselves to be seduced into bondage.

Because we allow ourselves to be enslaved to systems, programs, traditions, religion and folks, the enemy sits back laughing because he has us just where he wants us.

We are too enslaved to be free because of distractions that ensnare us, that keep us from enjoying the freedom we have been given to be who we are, what we are, and carry out why we exist.

Why do we continue to play that same ole blue slave song in our life?

You know the one:

"Your freedom is gone, baby. And you are unable to be yourself. You can't fulfill your purpose, child, because the real you don't live here."

If you're handcuffed in your mind, how can you actively walk in your purpose?

You were not created to be a living soul to be imprisoned. You were created to be free.

Why are we, especially those of us in the body of

Christ and those who attend church, more bound than people who operate in the world?

Could it be that we have a form of godliness but we deny the power thereof?

Could it be that we are so busy trying to wash the sinner's face and let our faces remain dirty, telling ourselves that it's ok because we are in the church?

Could it be that Maybelline, Max Factor, Mary Kay, and Mac have so concealed and covered us up that we only see our made-up reflection instead of the image of Christ within us?

Do we sugar-coat, water down, gloss over, skip around, and dodge God's truth about us so much that we cannot recognize the freedom we have?

We are so busy speaking in tongues, trying to shout our way out, preaching to and counseling each other, that the real truth that brings change escapes us?

I'm just asking.

Why is the body of Christ in such bondage?

How can we help free the captive when we are imprisoned?

We have bonded with an illusion of truth instead of the real thing.

Truth mixed with lies and deceit is no longer truth but deception.

We are an illusion of truth and continue to birth this illusion.

We really have a false image of Christ which in turn gives us a false image of ourselves.

Our understanding of our purpose is distorted and disfigured because it is contaminated with lies and half-truths.

Freedom without truth is like salvation without Jesus.

It's a lie that will ultimately kill and bring damnation to us.

What is truth?

Truth is the actual state of a matter, an allegiance

with fact or reality.

Truth is a verified and indisputable principle.

Truth is *not* an opinion, a perception, or a system of beliefs.

Opinions, perceptions, and belief systems can be true in your mind's eye, but can be proven, factual, boldfaced lies.

Just because you choose to believe and live by an opinion, a perception, or a belief does not make it true.

God is Truth.

Jesus said, "I am the Way, the Truth and the Life".

When you unveil the truth, you unveil yourself.

When you immerse yourself in truth you discover more about who you are, what you are, and why you are here.

You are a mystery hidden in the truth of God waiting to be unraveled.

The enemy and lies want to keep you ignorant about your mysteriousness to distract you from unveiling your true identity.

Once you trust Jesus as your Savior and Lord you will know more and more of your undiscovered self.

Let me pause for a minute to explain what I mean about trusting Jesus Christ as your Lord and Savior.

Once we accept the fact that Jesus Christ made it possible for us to no longer walk around feeling guilty about having to do anything to make up for all we have done, are doing, and will do, we are given an unparalleled opportunity to be who we are, what we are, and experience why we exist—now that's shouting news.

Because of Christ, we no longer need to feel burdened down because of accusations and condemnation from others (natural or supernatural).

There is no longer a need to feel weighted down by the sense that we are in trouble for anything. We are free—free to be.

See, there is so much more to salvation than fire

insurance. Read your policy—the bible.

Christianity teaches us to get saved—believing who, what, and why Jesus is—so we can go to heaven when we die.

That is all good and true.

But, before we die, we have a life to live while here on earth.

So, what can that life on earth look like?

Jesus didn't die so we could live defeated, depressed, dead lives here on earth.

The devil is a lie.

Jesus came to give us life more abundantly.

As a believer, an abundant life awaits us, here on earth.

Do you know what abundance means?

Abundance indicates that we are in a plentiful, lavish, overflowing, and inexhaustible state.

It doesn't just mean money—though you can have an abundant supply of money or a full bank account to boot.

Believers can be rich monetarily.

There is nothing wrong with being rich as long as it is not preventing you from allowing your spirit to flourish while on earth.

Use your riches for yourself and to help others as your purpose dictates.

Abundance applies not only to riches. It includes joy, peace, love, etc.

We have more than enough resources—materially and spiritually—for ourselves and to share with those in our sphere of influence.

When abundance exists, we have an overflow.

Live in the overflow of God.

Do you want an overflow in your life?

Imagine filling a glass with water.

The water reaches the rim of the glass.

As you keep pouring, the water begins to spill—flowing over the top and down the sides of the glass moving, and spreading this way and that until the surface under the glass is covered by the water.

The water starts to drip on the floor, trickling over.

Now, you have more than enough water.

You now have an overflow.

Water flows.

It moves, streams, glides over, and around.

Even when bottled it does not allow the container to hinder its function.

It still operates in its purpose of movement by causing waves, quenching thirst, and making things clean.

That's the way our lives are to be in Christ—abundant—an overflow of every promise, an overflow of resources, an overflow of wealth, an overflow of joy, peace, and love.

A life where there is nothing broken, missing, or lacking.

If we consciously live in the abundance God has

given us, we become less greedy, unselfish, less hateful, less troubled, and more positive.

When we live in the overflow, love spills out of us.

We operate in peace instead of bondage, restriction, and fear.

When we find ourselves restricted and in bondage, why do we forget that we are free?

Why do we stop doing what we are created to do?

We revert to behaving cowardly.

We stop praising God.

We don't pray.

We quit studying THE WORD.

We give up on God, abandon ourselves, and shutdown on fulfilling our purpose.

We stop being who we are.

We stop being what we are.

We turn a deaf ear to why we are here.

We become imposters—no longer being our real selves.

Let me tell you something, people of God.

We are not designed to quit.

God does not quit on us, so, don't dare quit on Him or yourself.

If you stop and refuse to walk through your purpose process and step into your assigned place, if you decide to lay down to die, if you choose to commit spiritual suicide, you are not only killing yourself, you are committing homicide as well.

You kill all the folks assigned to your life.

See, this kingdom assignment is not all about you.

It is tied to other people in your sphere of influence.

So, whether you feel like it or not, want to or don't want to, the truth of the matter is, you must allow yourself to be who you are, what you are, and fulfill the reason you exist.

Get up off your "blessed assurance" and tell the devil or whatever has put you in this place of giving up to back up off of you.

Serve notice that the poisonous lies being whispered in your ears and mind no longer work.

Declare that every plot, plan, trick, scheme, and illusion designed to kill you is now null and void in Jesus' name.

By doing this, the lies cannot continue to bind you, unless you choose to let them.

The lies have only as much power as you give them.

Take back your power.

You are wonderfully made.

You are a vessel full of tremendous power.

Stop giving your power away by letting what people say about you affect and infect you.

The truth about you is the only thing that matters.

What God has declared about you—who you are, what you are, and why you exist—is the only meaningful thing you need to know.

You are an awesome spirit in a wonderfully made body.

So, stop releasing your power from bed-to-bed with folks who are spiritual assassins.

Stop yoking up and creating soul ties in the spirit realm by relinquishing yourself spiritually and sexually—allowing things to be deposited inside of you that don't synch up with who you are, what you are, and why you exist.

Cut the ties now.

Stop allowing men and women to buy you.

Stop selling yourself.

Stop prostituting your mind, body, and soul.

You are not an object that folks can put on a lay-a-way plan making monthly payments.

Baby, you are much more than that.

That lay-a-way plan means just that.

Folks will lay you away, keep you hidden, keep you out of sight, ease over and make a payment here and there by bedding you down.

You may get some of your bills paid, a wad of cash,

or a pretense of fringe benefits.

But, know this; it will cost you—stripping you of your true identity.

Oh, I know right now it looks as if you have the upper hand feeling like you're not being used.

You may be saying this, "You've got to give a little to get a little."

While that may be your opinion, perception, or belief for the moment, it is not God's truth about you.

See, men and women, you are much more than a low-budget whore or a high-class prostitute.

Well, what is the difference, Cristi?

Not much, really.

As a low-budget whore, you sell yourself cheap.

The toys you receive for your tricks are not name-brand, but they are costly to your soul.

A few clothes from Penney's, a happy meal here and there, and a pimped out car does it for you.

As a high-class prostitute, you also sell yourself

cheap. But, your toys and trinkets are more expensive.

A few trips, designer clothes, couture handbags, jewelry, and a Jag, might do it for you. But it's costly to your soul, nonetheless.

Whore sounds more derogatory than prostitute does it not?

Nevertheless, they mean the same thing.

You just choose the name you answer to.

The whore and the prostitute answer to different names but they have a lot in common.

The handcuffs of bondage have them tied to the call and locked to the name.

After you receive your payments, the shame and the self-deprecation flood your soul.

You may be saying that you don't feel shame or cheapened, but you do, don't you?

And believe it or not, it becomes evident in other ways.

Cristi, are you judging?

No, I'm freeing you.

I'm truthing *(my made up word)* you.

Lord knows I have vices. We all do.

We all have stuff imprisoning and handcuffing us.

But, honey, freedom awaits us all.

Freedom begins with our relationship with God and a renewed mind.

Can you see yourself free?

Free to be yourself?

Free to be, spirit?

Freedom is not a penalty but a privilege.

You have the right to be free.

You are created to be free.

Jesus paid the price for your freedom.

Since you are free to be your wonderful self, that's why you are not to allow folks to put you on lay-a-way plans or any other type of plan to be purchased, bought, and pimped out.

Now that you have freedom in knowing who you are,

what you are, and why you exist, tell those people and systems that come around trying to buy you these words: "I am not lay-a-way-able. You can't debit, credit, or charge me because I'm not for sale. I've already been purchased by One higher than you. I'm extremely costly.

"I'm so valuable that it took a cross, a death, a burial, and a resurrection to purchase me so that I can live out my freedom.

"Jesus Christ's nail prints are the receipt. His blood purchased me, paid for me, and packaged me for freedom. So, I'm *not* for sale."

Glory to God!

We've already been stamped "Paid in Full" and sealed with the Holy Ghost.

It's time that we rise and walk in total liberty, in absolute freedom.

Too often we look for outward signs of our freedom before we begin to see ourselves as free people.

Can I tell you this?

Seeing outward manifestations of freedom is not how it works.

First, you need to look inside yourself to see your freedom

Then, believe that you are free.

After you do this, demonstrated freedom will appear.

You are already free.

Your spirit—the real you—is free.

Remember, spirit can't be contained or limited.

When there is an awakening in your spirit to truth, your outward form has to align with this truth.

Once we are awakened to the truth that we are free, the handcuffs of bondage—i.e., pride, greed, fornication, homosexuality, lust, lies, shame, low self-esteem, residuals of molestation, trauma from rape, drunkenness, prostitution, whoredom, shop-a-holism depression, deception, condemnation, death, etc.—have to fall off of us.

Jesus paid the price for these handcuffs of bondage to be broken.

Since He paid the price, there's nothing that we have to pay.

We simply accept that we're no longer chained to the vices of bondage because we're free.

John 8:36 reads, "Therefore, if the Son makes you free, you shall be free indeed."

Because Jesus Christ, the Son, has made us free, we've been liberated from death (disconnection) associated with sin (deliberate disobedience to the known will of God).

We're released from the penalty of sin—disconnection from God as a consequence of our deliberate disobedience to His known will.

So, Cristi, are you telling me that Jesus Christ came and paid the price for me to be free in my spirit?

Yes.

Jesus came to pay the penalty of our sin—our

disconnection from God as a result of our intentional disobedience to His known will—past, present, and future.

Our spirit is truly free to operate in the body that God created for us—giving us overwhelming freedom and choice to be our true selves without restriction and limitation.

Before Jesus' costly payment on the cross, our spirit was in captivity because of a spiritual law which demanded such an extremely huge payment.

Humankind was constantly hounded by spiritual bill collectors because Adam deliberately disobeyed God's known will long ago. The spiritual debt rested upon all of us.

The odd thing is, we were (are) unable to pay that debt—no matter how good we tried or try to behave, how many animals we took before the priests for sacrifice, or how many times we attend(ed) church service.

Nothing canceled this spiritual debt that disconnected us from God because Adam deliberately disobeyed God's known will.

When I say nothing, I mean nothing.

So, when Jesus Christ died on the cross, He canceled this long outstanding spiritual debt—once and for all.

John 19:28 and 30 communicate clearly, "···Jesus, knowing that all things were now accomplished, that the Scripture might be fulfilled···He [Jesus] said, 'It is finished!' And bowing His head, He gave up His spirit."

Since the spiritual bill collectors have been paid by Jesus, now, our conscience is clear.

We are free to be who we're created to be, free to do what we're created to do, and free to live out our purpose for this appointed time, which is why we're here.

Now that we have liberty and freedom—walk in it.

We really are clueless about who we are in Christ Jesus.

To know we are free and still choose to be in bondage is really self-imprisonment.

We put ourselves behind prison bars waiting for someone to release us when we've already been released—set free.

We are the prison guards holding the keys to our self-built cells.

It's insanity at its best.

We are free people behaving like locked up inmates.

Some bible versions state, "Whom the Son sets free is free indeed."

I love that.

To set something means to position it.

The cross positioned us for freedom on earth.

I also believe another positioning took place in our predetermined state.

When God reached inside Himself and pulled out our spirit, He formed us and breathed the breath of His Spirit into all humankind.

He placed us in our momma's womb for a set purpose, for a set time to accomplish his set will for our life.

God set you up to display His glory.

He set you up for greatness.

He set you up for a divine purpose.

And He set you up for freedom.

You exist to be free, to be your real self, and to bring freedom to others.

Your purpose demands freedom.

If you are in bondage, so is the purpose inside of you.

Have you ever found yourself shifting from job to job?

Moving from one relationship to another?

Searching for acceptance over here and trying to appease folks over there?

Have you found yourself in places you didn't really want to be?

Have you been in situations without peace? Working somewhere but feeling very restless? Are you in a discontent marriage?

Or in the midst of an existence where peace is absent?

I've been there a lot.

To be honest with you, when I turned forty-four last year, I just started to enter my place of rest—my place of peace.

A place of rest and ease is your place of peace.

In this place of peace, you come to a position in your life where you are at ease with who you are.

You no longer try to live up to other people's expectations.

Traditions imposed by religion, rules and regulations, momma's and daddy's dreams, being the perfectionist, faking and pretending to be somebody other than yourself, going through the motions of living, and trying to live up to your own restrictive self-imposed philosophies just seem to fall off of you.

Don't you want to experience that place of rest—that place of peace?

Do I fully reside in that place of complete rest, total peace?

No, but I can tell you that I have entered that place.

I am experiencing it more and more as each day goes by.

It feels absolutely wonderful.

When the bands of outwardly imposed expectations start falling off of you, you start to live and breathe only the breath God placed in you.

Living to please Him by being who you are, what you are, and expressing why you are here, snaps the cords of freedom.

You find yourself on a journey to a place called rest—a place called peace.

You start to see that other people's words, ideas, and negativity are just tools the enemy uses to assassinate your assignment.

I want to get the message across clearly that the enemy is a duplicator.

Everything God does, the enemy tries to do.

Have there been people in your life who try to get close to you to steal your identity?

When you do something, they try to do the same thing?

As you freely exercise who you are, they feel the need to replicate it—duplicating and imitating your every move?

I'm not referring to a "first grader copycat" kind of thing.

I'm talking about something much more sinister and demonic—a familiar spirit, so to speak.

There have been people in my life who've tried to duplicate and imitate me.

So much so, I really didn't know who I was anymore.

This imposter is tiring, draining, and distracting.

That thing—that sinister, demonic, familiar spirit attached to that person—is assigned to your life by the enemy to tire you out, drain you, and distract you so you will not fulfill your purpose on earth.

I didn't always see this duplicating and imitating for what it really was.

When I noticed the creepiness of the spirit's actions, I became very angry.

Like I said, I just called the person a copycat until God began to expose the true nature of the sinister, demonic, familiar spirit attached to them.

It was assigned to me to thwart out who I am, what I am, and why I exist.

This particular familiar spirit wraps itself in coyness.

It pretends to be your friend or desires closeness to you because it wants to try to be like you.

It works out of a sugary sweetness bathed in manipulation seducing you into a false sense of security and trust.

Then it strikes.

It starts to dress like you, act like you, and even talk like you.

People sometimes mistake this spirit to be you.

It causes you to think everybody is against you so you'll become dependent upon it—this imitator, this imposter.

It operates in deceit, trickery, and false love because it wants to be you.

It wants to take your life.

This spirit is full of greed.

It uses you.

It's very judgmental.

It does anything to make a dollar.

It's intelligent and sneaky.

It saps you of your strength.

It strips you of your identity if you are not careful.

Ultimately, its goal is to latch on to you to destroy your purpose by trying to make your vision its own.

Once it infiltrates, it's hard to find a door of escape from its web because its goal is to entrap and ensnare you.

I had to pray my way out from under this spirit's control and disconnect from those people the enemy sent to steal my identity.

Can I tell you this?

I am now free from them.

I allowed this spirit to enter my presence through a wide opened door called low self-esteem. Thinking that I needed someone to help me fulfill the purpose God placed inside of me.

Instantly, I knew I should have gone to the purpose giver Himself, God—who always stands by to aid me instead of looking to someone else for reassurance and validation.

Insecurity will do that to you. You know?

I wouldn't trade the experience for anything because it was part of the process in fulfilling my purpose.

A part of why I exist.

After my encounter with this imitating spirit, I became stronger.

I am constantly redefining myself through change.

I no longer answer to lack by looking to people to help fill voids within me.

I go to God asking Him to fill the voids with His Holy Spirit.

What are you saying Cristi?

I am saying, be careful who you connect with.

I'm not saying we do not need people in our lives because we do.

Just because someone is with you does not mean they have your best interest at heart contrary to what they tell you.

I shared with you earlier that the enemy is a duplicator.

Just as God has a set up for you, so does the enemy.

You must become wise to the enemy's tactics and

antics.

Don't allow him to set you up because his setup is to cause you to fail, fall, and forget.

He wants to stop you from fulfilling your purpose.

He uses imps, demons, cohorts, devices, plots, plans, schemes, tricks, folks, church, religion, friends, foes, pastors, prophets, teachers, apostles, evangelists, co-workers, husbands, wives, mothers, fathers, children, uncles, aunts, sister, brothers, teachers, etc.

His mission is to kill the assignment in you.

Don't become a casualty in this spiritual war, especially when you don't have to.

A most crucial part of accurately identifying who you are, what you are, and why you exist is to establish a relationship with God through Christ.

If you've never reconnected with God, if you do not know Jesus as your Savior and Lord, you can.

God wants a personal relationship with you.

It's not hard.

Romans 10:9-10 reads, "···if you confess with your mouth the Lord Jesus and believe in your heart that God has raised Him from the dead, you will be saved.

"For with the heart one believes unto righteousness, and with the mouth confession is made unto salvation."

You can become free by knowing the one who purchased your freedom—Christ.

To reconnect with God, our heavenly Father, believe and accept who Jesus is, what Jesus is, and why Jesus exists.

God loves you so much and wants a relationship with you.

This action connects you back to your original state, your true essence, your true self—your spirit.

If you desire to have a relationship with Him so you can fully live out who you are, what you are, and why you are here, just open your mouth and tell God what's in your heart.

He is listening. I promise.

I feel led by the Spirit of God to insert how I asked for a relationship with Him through Christ Jesus.

I said this aloud:

Lord, I believe that you are the Son of God. I believe that you died for my sins, and that God raised you from the dead. Forgive me for my sins. Come into my heart. I desire a relationship with you, Amen.

Glory to God, salvation is available to all of us. When Jesus saves you, He frees you not only from the flames of an eternal hell.

But, He also frees you from every form of bondage in your life and allows you to experience the abundance he promised.

That's what salvation for a Christian does.

It preserves you from destruction and evil allowing you to experience your true self.

As stated previously, Jesus Christ already paid the

spiritual debt collector hounding every person who doesn't know why they are weighted down with a guilty conscious resulting from one man's (Adam's) actions, long ago, of deliberately disobeying God's known will, which caused a disconnect between God and humans.

When Jesus hung on the cross, He said, "It is finished."

We must learn to rest in the finished work of Christ.

When we do, we'll stop pimpin' Him for stuff and stop trying to buy, shout, and glide our way into the Kingdom of Heaven.

We'll stop being spiritual prostitutes—selling our gifts and anointing for fame, glamour, and recognition.

Oh, yeah, we will.

May I just humbly submit something to you?

In the body of Christ, we've become a bunch of Slick Willies, pimping ourselves and prostituting our flocks out to a bunch of other Slick Willies that fleece the flock with a sugar-coating truth.

Is it any wonder that we remain puzzled that the people continue in bondage?

People are still in bondage because they come to your church seeking Jesus and truth to walk in their freedom.

Instead they enter into deceit, tricks, illusions, and lies.

Not only do they bring their already full baggage with them when they enter your church, now, you've opened their bags stuffing other hindrances into them causing their bondage to be even more severe.

Their luggage is heavier than before.

Instead of receiving liberty, they received more oppression.

How can we set the captives free when many of us who are trying to do the setting are still captive ourselves?

What does captive mean?

Enslaved, forcibly confined, kept under controlled restraint and, held in bondage.

Are you a captive?

What and who is enslaving you?

Has religion placed you in bondage?

Do rules, regulations, and traditions imprison you?

Are you a prisoner to people's perceptions of you?

Are you handcuffed to your pastor instead of being linked with Jesus?

Come on now, be honest with yourself.

Some readers may think I'm anti-church, anti-order, or anti-protocol.

I assure you that I'm not.

I'm Anti-Deception.

I've walked through hell's flames of deception seeking the truth.

It almost killed me but it didn't.

God mandated me to blow the trumpet, to ring the alarm, to cry aloud, to spare not, and warn His people.

I cannot, will not compromise any longer.

God's not pleased with the fluff of nothingness being spewed across the pulpits.

It's not His truth.

Instead of pulpits pulling people out of their pits, the enemy is using pulpits to pull people deeper into the pit—straight into a pit of living hell, a pit of bondage.

Our way to freedom is through Christ and His truth.

When we accept this, the bands of bondage are broken and freedom is attainable.

When shackles from your mind loosen, and you start to soar in your divine purpose carrying out the accompanying assignments, you'll begin to experience true free.

When you clearly begin to see your true self—your real essence, the genuine you, your spirit—you embark upon your freedom walk.

When you stop striving, running around in circles, searching for what you already have, then freedom becomes your way of life.

Wow, God is so awesome.

He didn't create us to try.

He created us to be.

The enemy sold us the lie of trying.

Do you know what the word trying implies? You may be shocked.

The word "trying" gives the impression of straining, hardship, distress, annoyance, upset, difficulty, hard to endure, not easy, irritating, nerve racking, taxing, tough, exasperating, tiresome, wearisome, bothersome, troublesome, irking, vexing, aggravating, strangulating.

I told you that trying is not quite what you expected. Is it?

Yet, this is how the majority of us live—in a trying mode.

Whether a believer in Christ or not, churched or un-churched, black, white, or other, male or female, rich or poor, we are all trying—trying to get more, trying to be better, trying to strive harder, trying to live right, trying to develop or maintain our relationships, trying to be great parents, trying to be good spouses, etc.

It's exhausting.

When we're asked how we're doing, we frequently respond like this. "I'm trying to stay alive." Or "I'm trying to make it."

Church folks say, "I'm trying to pray."

"I'm trying to worship."

"I'm trying to praise."

"I'm trying to live holy."

"I'm trying to read my bible."

"I'm trying to fulfill my purpose."

"I'm trying to be delivered."

"I'm trying to be saved."

"I'm trying to live in integrity."

I'm trying has become a mantra for many of us. We're so busy trying that we're not BE-coming. God really began to deal with me about the concept of trying to release me into my freedom.

Our words are powerful, carrying weight, either negative or positive.

When we say that we are trying, we speak negative things over our lives like annoyance, upset, aggravation, strangulation, and all the other descriptions I listed earlier.

We've spoken something God never spoke.

If we are speaking things God hasn't spoken, then whose words are we using?

Whose voice are we listening to?

Jesus said, "My sheep know my voice and a stranger they will NOT follow."

Lately, I've become so sick and tired of trying.

Recently, in a 3 a.m. prayer, I heard these words in my spirit, *"I never created you to try.*

"I created you to be."

God said, *"Stop trying and just be.*

"When you finally drop the try *from trying you only*

have the –ing.

"When you add 'be' *in front of* –ing, *the trying changes to being.*

"I created you as a spirit being.

"Be spirit.

"Be you, the real you.

"Nothing in your spirit has to try.

"Spirit simply has to be.

"Do not try to worship—BE worship.

"Do not try to live the scriptures—BE the scriptures

"Do not try to act holy—BE holy.

"Do not try to be delivered—BE delivered.

"Do not try to go to church—BE the church.

"Do not try to get saved—BE saved.

"Do not try to live in your purpose—BE your purpose."

We often think the scripture means following physically.

But it also means following spiritually.

You can follow strange voices even in your mind.

You can have dialogs and conversations in your mind with the enemy as well as your own vain imaginations.

The conversations in your mind affect your words and your words affect your life.

When you begin to listen to and speak a language other than God's language, you eat the fruit of your spoken word.

Believe you are who God says you are.

Roll those thoughts around in your mind.

Speak those things.

Release them into the atmosphere.

Walk in the realm of being.

The Nike slogan says, "Just Do It".

The Kingdom says, "Just BE!"

Your spirit is already, inclined, and prepared to be.

When your spirit awakens to the knowledge that you no longer have an age old burdensome debt to pay to a harassing spiritual debt collector because one man disobeyed God's known will, which disconnected humankind from God, your spirit comes fully alive to its predetermined state.

Your spirit allows you to become more aware of who you are, what you are, and why you exist.

Your spirit becomes responsive to its divinity, its position in Christ, its function within you.

Your spirit already knows it's been predisposed and prepared in the heavenlies.

Becoming aware of who you are, what you are, and why you exist, your spirit aligns with your earthly consciousness allowing you to walk in this awesome knowledge and freedom.

Your spirit knows it's complete, eager to do the right thing, and manifests its purpose.

Your spirit is willing to be holy—following God, loving yourself plus others, and flowing in its freedom to be.

Your outer self, the external you—the form you were given to house the real you—is spiritually weak.

Your body, your form, is not bad. It is just weak without your spirit operating it.

Your physical side can't truly follow your spirit until your spirit has a godly awakening and takes its rightful position.

Your body, mind, thoughts, appetites, etc., yield to your spirit when it is in control.

Question: Who's guiding you?

Is it your spirit—the real you—or your physical-self (your form) made up of various appetites, devices, and thoughts?

Come on let's take a test to examine ourselves.

Do you have an intimate relationship with God?

Do you have a renewed mind?

Are you being obedient to the voice of God?

Do you believe His promises concerning you are yes and amen?

Do you listen to your spirit?

What is your speech like?

Do you speak blessings one second and speak curses the next?

So far, how would you grade yourself?

There are a lot of questions on the test, but I will stop here.

I encourage you to examine your life.

Look at your fruit.

What are you producing with your thoughts, speech, actions, and feelings?

Are you moving in your spirit or have you become motionless in your nature without an awakened spirit?

You are not to become stationary or entrapped. You were created for movement and constant renewal of your mind impacting those around you to become aware of their greatness allowing your breath to flow so your purpose is evident on earth.

Jesus moved in the womb, and He moved out of the

tomb.

Neither place entrapped Him.

Neither place immobilized Him.

Places of concealment became places of freedom because Jesus broke forth moving about to fulfill His purpose.

Concealment is not always a bad thing.

When a concealed thing kisses the time of revelation, an unveiling springs forth.

There will be a showing.

Jesus was concealed in the womb and in the tomb.

When time kissed His revealing, He was unveiled on earth.

From the womb, He came forth to fulfill the prophets, "unto us a child is born, unto us a son is given."

From the tomb, He fulfilled scripture as being Savior of the world setting the captive free.

Jesus was publicly displayed.

He could not stay in confinement because He *is* freedom—free to be all He is, free to move about in all of His glory.

His public display also made each of us free to be our true selves displaying our glory.

Let me tell you this.

It's time for your *Coming-Out* party.

The location's been picked.

Invitations sent.

And your guests have arrived.

The party isn't a party until the guest of honor arrives.

So, come on out.

No longer allow anything or anyone, natural or supernatural, to cause you to retreat.

It's timeout for fear, shame, or whatever to keep you hidden.

Concealing yourself because of your past is no longer acceptable.

Break free of low-budget thinking that's trying to keep you in bondage to secrecy.

This is your *Coming-Out* party.

There's no longer a need for you to let people keep you down feeding you their plans and ideas for your life.

You are free to feast on the Breasted One, Jesus Christ, instead of sucking on the nipples of humankind, which cause you to eat contamination poisoning you and stunting your growth.

You are now free to come out of the womb that was created to nourish, protect, and birth you for a season.

You no longer have to be womb-trapped.

The womb is contracting to set you free. But you don't want to be delivered.

When this happens, the place that once concealed and protected you has now become a death trap for you instead.

You experience a lack of oxygen causing retardation.

Retarded isn't a word that I like to use but the Holy Ghost says to speak it because we really have the wrong concept of the word when it comes to our spirituality.

Retardation causes slow movement, delayed growth, hindrance, awkwardness, and ineffectiveness in some form or fashion.

Are you getting it?

We are suffering not so much from brain damage but spiritual damage.

Spiritual Retardation Disorder is running amuck in our lives because we will not allow our spirits to awaken.

Oh, we may allow partial awakenings in our spirits, but, not to the point of coming into the full knowledge of God's truth.

Churches can't awaken you.

Pastors can't awaken you.

Religion can't awaken you.

Jumping over pews, shouting throughout the church, and running around the building can't awaken you.

Don't get me wrong, all these things can give you a façade of being spiritually awakened.

God is not looking for partial awakenings.

He is looking for your spirit to have a full awakening to who He is, what He is, and why He is.

It is a true relationship with God, knowing and believing the truth about Him, that causes your spirit, your real identity, to become fully alive.

The true gospel of Christ is not being preached.

We're not having the truth of God being taught to us.

We're only hearing half, incomplete truths—being partially changed. We are spiritually, alive in some parts and dead in others.

All across this nation we're behaving like lifeless spiritual fetuses.

When God reach inside Him to pull your spirit out of His, breathed you into your momma's womb, you were spirit in the form of a fetus.

You were alive.

I'm about to use some strong language that might make you somewhat squeamish.

So, prepare yourself and know that I am operating under the authority of the Holy Spirit to release this information because relationships with God and purposes are at stake.

There're a lot of spiritual abortions being performed in our churches just like in the natural.

When abortion procedures are performed in the natural there are certain methods used to extract and kill the baby.

One frequently used abortion technique administered the first three months of a woman's pregnancy is known as the Salt Poisoning method, a.k.a. *Candy Apple Baby*.

Experts say a woman is injected directly into her amniotic sac—the fluid surrounding the baby—with a strong salt solution.

The baby inhales and ingests the poisoned solution generally causing the baby to struggle and convulse.

In about an hour's time, the baby dies.

The woman normally delivers the dead baby on that day or the next.

Why is the description *Candy Apple Baby* attached to this abortion technique?

The poisonous salt solution eats away the outer layer of the baby's skin leaving the baby's skin tissue with a red, glazed, raw look.

Cristi why insert this?

I'm inserting this because God says we have a lot of *Candy Apple Babies* in church.

We are being injected not with salt but with sugar.

We're being injected with a sugar-coated gospel, presented a sugar-coated Christ, and inhaling a sugar-coated doctrine.

When we inhale these sugar-coated things, we're

swallowing poison, which brings death to our spirit.

The amniotic sac, the foundational fluid designed to protect the church, is pierced with this sugar-coated gospel, Christ, and doctrine filled with lies, deceit, and strong delusions.

Like the *Candy Apple Baby*, we struggle, convulse, and die in the spiritual realm.

Our death is not happening in a day or two but slowly spans over years.

When injected by churches with a sugar-coated gospel, Christ, and doctrine, we are expelled into the world bearing no resemblance of our true identity.

We're similar to the burned, stripped, dead *Candy Apple Baby* having no likeness of a healthy newborn.

After receiving this sugar-coated gospel, Christ, and doctrine, we go out into the world administering our sugar-coated teaching to those who do not have a relationship with God.

We're ineffective in helping others become free to be

themselves.

All we give them is the same sweet syrupy sugar-coated substance we received, and it kills them.

Jesus didn't call us to be the sugar of the earth.

No, He called us to be the (non-poisonous) salt of the earth.

Jesus clearly states in Matthew 5:13, "You are the salt of the earth, but if the salt loses its flavor, how shall it be seasoned?

"It is then good for nothing but to be thrown out and trampled underfoot by men."

If all you ingest is sugar, you are in trouble.

Your spirit is about to go into shock, likely becoming a spiritual diabetic stuck in a coma with death looming over you.

Come alive.

Come out, people.

You're not a *Candy Apple Baby*.

You survived.

It's time to arise from your coma and enhance your flavor with some (non-poisonous) salt of God's truth to season this earth.

Another commonly used abortion technique is the *Suction* method.

With the *Suction* method, it's said that the woman's womb opening is paralyzed.

A hollow plastic tube with a knife-like tip is inserted into her uterus.

The tube is connected to a powerful pump with a *suction* force about exponentially more forceful than your home vacuum cleaner.

The baby's body is torn into pieces as it's sucked from the mother's body.

The hose frequently jerks as pieces of the baby become dislodged.

The placenta is cut from the inner wall of the mother's uterus.

The scraps are then sucked out into a bottle.

Abortions are not a pretty sight—neither in the natural nor the spiritual.

Suction is identified as a strong powerful force drawing you in.

The enemy of our soul is using people to suck us into all sorts of things.

The *Suction* method is prevalent in churches.

You may go to some people in the church for something, and they may have this *Suction* spirit attached to them—all the while they are plotting to abort you by drawing you into false gospels and strong delusions.

These spirits manipulate and trick.

They are full of deception with the goal to suck you out and kill you spiritually.

They are powerful. They have to be.

By design their technique is to paralyze and abort you—tugging at your beliefs, emptying you of the truth, and extrapolating Christ and your true identity out of you.

This spiritual abortionists paralyze you as their assistants use their plastic tubes with knife-like tips attached to the end inserting their deadly instruments into you.

With their powerful *suction* force, they pull out pieces of you dislodging your true identity until nothing but scarps of you are left.

Then they place you into bottles of confinement so you are no longer free to be the real you.

These spiritual abortionists and their assistants come in the forms of teachers, apostles, pastors, prophets, evangelists, ushers, gatekeepers, watchmen, family, friends, etc.

From the choir to the hospitality team, your spiritual enemy infiltrates to suck you out pulling you into death.

Many of us have fallen victim to the *Suction* method. The sad thing is we don't even realize it.

We've become immune to the sounds of the *Suction* devices.

We've become accustom to these powerful vacuum-cleaner-like mechanisms used by some churches (the places of gathering) that are trying to abort us.

When a vacuum cleaner is plugged into the right power source and used properly, it functions correctly by cleaning away debris and removing pieces that are just lying around.

It picks up the dirt and filth that create chaos.

When vacuum cleaners are used accurately they get into the crevices to suck up the litter.

The enemy's strategic plan is to unplug the spiritual vacuum-like apparatus, the church, completely from its true power source by disguising itself as the outlet.

The spiritual vacuum, originally designed to clear away rubbish, has plugged into some outlets that are not of God.

Some preachers are preaching a hollow plastic

gospel with a knife-like tip called lies attached to the tube of a powerful source called deception.

When the *Suction* tube is turned on, so is the deception.

We, the body of Christ, are sucked into utter darkness—just like the baby aborted using the *Suction* method.

We are torn into pieces as the *Suction* hose jerks us around trapping us in the enemy's snare allowing deception to kill us.

Unlike the fatally wounded babies who have no voice, we have a voice.

But, we've been silenced by powers of darkness and positions we hold in the church telling us not to speak out or scream.

It's time for the sinister sounds of *Suction* in our churches to STOP.

It's time for the voices of righteousness to rise up and silence the enemies.

A third abortion method God told me to write about is called *Partial Birth* abortions.

Partial Birth abortions are performed in the latter stages of pregnancy.

The woman's cervix is dilated allowing the entrance of forceps.

The foot or lower leg of the baby is located and pulled into the vagina.

Then the baby is pulled out in a breech position until the head is just inside the cervix with the baby's legs hanging outside the woman's body.

(This is hard to write!)

The baby's head is turned facedown as a pair of scissors plunge into the nape of his or her neck spreading open an enlarged wound. A suction tip is inserted into the gaping wound removing the baby's brain.

The tiny skull collapses and the dead baby is delivered.

In other words, the baby is alive, killed, and delivered completing the *Partial Birth* abortion process.

The enemy uses *Partial Birth* tactics to destroy and kill God's people.

We are in a breech position as our feet are pulled out dangling in the church while our heads are stuck in the cervix of the womb of the world.

Our desire is to walk with God and to exercise our freedom to be ourselves but our heads are stuck in the cervix of the world's system without a renewed mind and completely sealed off from fully knowing God.

We're not walking in freedom because we're stuck— stuck in positions ill-fitted for birthing and bringing forth life.

The enemy wants us to stay in a breeched position with our heads facedown.

Since our heads are stuck, lodged in with the things of the world, caught up in stuff not pertaining to God or our true identity—wedged in depression, ensnared by low self-esteem, entrapped in religion, webbed in deception, and framed in an untransformed mind—the enemy has us just where he wants us.

You go to church. Your feet dangle there, but you're stuck in homosexuality.

You hang around in the choir, but you're spellbound by crack.

You're cloaked in the ministry, but you're caught up in pimping and prostitution.

You wiggle your toes in the prophetic, but you're ensnared by pornography.

In this death looming breeched position, you're stuck and dangling.

This position is designed to suffocate you, to cut off your oxygen supply, and to kill you.

Where are the spiritual caretakers?

Where are the spiritual midwives designed to help guide you out so you can live?

Where are the spiritual doctors and assistants to

help turn and align you in the correct position for birth?

Where are the spiritually alive pastors, teachers, and leaders in the church?

Some are stuck themselves.

If they're in this death looming breeched position, how can they help you live?

Some are wielding scissors of deceit waiting for the arrival of sons and daughters to snuff out their lives simply because some children's birth becomes a threat to them.

They end up plunging the scissors of rejection into the nape of the partially born child's neck.

Though the womb is a vital place of growth before birth takes place, the enemy desires to make the womb your tomb—killing you before your delivery date.

The enemy is fine with you being conceived, but doesn't want you to be delivered with life in you.

Partial Birth abortions allow you to come out just a

little bit, but you're killed before full delivery.

Sometimes the church will allow you to come forth just a little, but will kill you before you can be delivered fully into your true self.

Can I tell you that sometimes you can't always trust the ones who're supposed to help deliver you?

At times, you can't believe the ones you see.

Instead of them using forceps to bring you into life, they just may be the ones holding the scissors behind their backs to plunge into the nape of your neck to kill you.

I'm not stating this to cause fear but to bring about awareness.

Become your own delivery instrument.

Be your own spiritual forceps by hearing the Holy Spirit leading and guiding you into your own deliverance.

When God delivers you, there's no need to worry about spiritually induced abortions—*Candy Apple*

Baby, Suction, Partial Birth, etc.

By developing a relationship with God, He's more than able to deliver you safely—placing you in your rightful position of purpose.

Why did God want to discuss these things about abortions?

He wants us to be aware that spiritual abortion methods are being performed daily to thwart us out so all He placed inside of us doesn't come forth into existence.

Our babies of purpose are being killed—murdered.

We allow enemies to trap us and shut us out of our purpose—sealing us into places of hopelessness.

We've strapped ourselves to abortion tables, all across this nation, in the form of religion, pews, people, and self-doubt.

We yield our bodies, minds, and spirits to folks that will use any viable instrument to terminate us.

We allow them to c-section, drug, and induce us into

false labor causing untimely births.

Some babies of purpose are stillborn.

Some are overdue.

Where is your baby?

Where is your purpose?

Were you forced to deliver too soon before the gestation period of your purpose was complete?

Did you push too soon because of your eagerness instead of holding?

Was your purpose expelled before its time because the contractions were too painful?

Is your baby of purpose a preemie?

It's often very difficult for something born prematurely to survive.

Premature babies usually have a low birth weight, are under nourished, and sometimes have mental disorders impairing their hearing, sight, speech, mind, and movement.

I've prematurely delivered babies in the natural and

in the spirit.

As a matter of fact, all of my natural children were born prematurely.

Thank God, by His grace, they're alive and well with no birth defects.

Have you delivered a stillborn purpose?

Spiritually speaking, we sometimes carry stuff void of life producing purpose.

We think just because our spiritual baby is leaping, kicking, and our purpose sounds great, that it has life—not so, my friend.

If something appears lively with movement, that doesn't mean it's living.

There are a lot of things and people appearing to be alive, but they're dead.

We all appear to be living, but many of us are just surviving—big difference.

Sometimes God allows miscarriages in more ways than pregnancy.

Have you experienced a spiritual miscarriage of your purpose?

We have miscarriages in our marriages, our walk with God and our relationships with people.

From time-to-time, we have miscarriages when it comes to the word of God.

Not fulfilling our purpose is a form of miscarriage.

We carry things wrong.

We fail in transporting.

We carry amiss with impure motives.

When your purpose is born, it has your heart, your nature, and your character.

When you have a kingdom assignment, your agenda aligns with the kingdom, as well.

Just because you have a miscarriage doesn't mean you can't conceive again.

Is your baby of purpose overdue?

Have you waited a long time to give birth?

Is your baby stuck in your womb—lying dormant?

Sometimes it feels like we're never going to give birth to the dreams and visions God placed within us.

With God, timing is so important.

When God's timing (Kairos) kisses the world's timing (Chronos), the spiritual timing of purpose manifests.

Sometimes what other people label overdue may just be on time.

I encourage you, don't stop dreaming, believing, or pushing simply because your baby of purpose is secured in time.

Time your contractions.

Align yourself in harmony with God's will.

Unlock the space accommodating the right moment of your purpose by synching with Kairos and Chronos shouting, *"IT'S TIME!"*

Let me say it again.

There's a specific time for the appearance of everything God placed in you.

You are an awesome vessel of God.

He empowers you to impact His kingdom through your purpose.

The time is NOW.

I know the enemy, people, and even you have tried to disrobe you of your priestly garments.

But, baby, let me tell you, your robe of righteousness awaits you.

No longer do you have to be a locked up vessel sitting on a shelf collecting dust.

You have treasure—the real you—in your earthen vessel waiting to be unveiled.

Let your true essence break forth.

I hear the Lord saying, *"There is a release springing forth out of you."*

Even as you read this book, God is releasing you from restraints that have hindered you for too long.

He's not only releasing you. He's releasing Himself inside of you—filling your awakened spirit with His Spirit.

God says, *"Release simply means to set free.*

"Your penalties have already been paid.

"You have been granted immunity.

"Will you accept it?"

Jesus paid the price for you.

Freedom belongs to you.

He's setting you free from the snares of the enemy.

He's liberating you from hurt.

He's discharging you from pain.

Accept His release.

He's releasing you from that physical abortion you had, that adulterous lifestyle you live, that pride that puffs you up, that low self-esteem weighing you down, and that shame which has attached itself to you.

Accept His release.

He's releasing you from manipulation others use against you, and you use against others.

He's releasing you from the stench of greed on you, those drugs keeping you in a cloud of confusion distorting your view, and deceit that leads you into all kinds of traps.

Accept His release.

He's releasing you from depression that's keeping you hidden, that hopelessness walling you in, those opinions contrary to the truth, and from folks hindering you.

Accept His release.

He's yoking you with your spirit.

He's releasing you from traditions continuing to blind you to what is new, religious suppression, façades hiding your true identity, hatred that builds walls around you shutting you in, and every trap set up to capture and hold you.

God says He is releasing you.

Accept His release.

Millions of us are trapped, captured, caught, sealed off, and ensnared like caged animals desiring freedom.

We're trapped in our homes, on our jobs, in our

churches, in our relationships, in abuse, in pornography, in our thinking, in the way we love, in confusion, in our mindsets, in anger, in sadness, in loneliness, in our past, in our present, in outdated beliefs of no future, and in ourselves.

Because we can't see our way out, we become immobilized screaming, "CAN ANYBODY SEE ME? I AM TRAPPED!"

If we stay trapped too long, the trap becomes our dwelling place, our residence, and a familiar place of comfort.

Soon, we become our traps—looking and speaking like them.

These traps dictate our lives because we've become one with them.

Traps are indiscriminate.

They don't care who we are, what position we hold, or what title we wear.

We've all found ourselves in some trapped places at

some point in our living.

Whether they are traps set by people, the enemy, or us out of foolishness and pride.

You wouldn't believe how many pastors, priests, Sunday school teachers, parents, children, congressmen, Presidents, athletes, etc. feel trapped.

Traps don't care about your race, sex, religion, or socio-economic status.

Believe it or not, there is a trap with your name on it.

Oh, but the good news is, there's a trap door called Jesus.

When you open the door discovering who He is and your relationship with Him progresses, your trap's hold loosens—allowing you to walk into freedom.

Some of us have become incarcerated in our minds— imprisoned to a systematic way of thinking instead of a spiritual way of reasoning.

Therefore, we're held hostage in our mind because of the way we view things. This in turn binds us in our living.

In the United States, we have the wonderful privilege of being a very open-minded country.

As U.S. citizens, we have freedoms only some countries dream about.

However, as a nation with all of our liberties, have we become even more enslaved?

Orderly function, instead of chaotic operating systems, is great.

Nevertheless, we've become a society so organized in procedures and protocols, originally designed to bring order and freedom, until we've created an even more confused and enslaved world in which we live.

We're free to live wherever we want, do what we please, marry whomever we choose.

However, in this great land of liberty, I believe true freedom eludes us.

Have we become incarcerated to freedom itself?

I want you to know this.

True freedom and liberty does exist. And all of us can experience it.

In freedom, the handcuffs of bondage snap off allowing the liberating strength of freedom to lift us far above the ashes of immorality, degradation, and disillusionment.

Anytime your freedom involves an ounce of compromise it's no longer freedom, but bondage.

Truth mixed with lies is no longer truth.

Freedom without truth is death.

We don't have real freedom without truth.

And we don't have truth without freedom.

One without the other is bondage.

Life doesn't reside in bondage, entrapment, or an imprisoned state of being—only death for a dying soul.

You, my friend, were created to *LIVE*—*to Live in Victory Endlessly.*

I just heard the spirit of God tell me that.

When you begin to **LIVE**, you begin to be.

When you begin to be, you begin to **LIVE**.

You have this awesome potential in you.

It's time for you to release it so God's glory inside of you can be displayed.

Even though you were caught in some terrible traps, you weren't killed, praise God.

The very fact that you're reading this book tells me, and prayerfully you, that God's plan and purpose for your life still remain.

I don't care what it looks like, right now, what it seems like, or even what it feels like in your present moment.

You're meant to be here.

You have a purpose to fulfill because you're still standing.

If you will, take a moment to soak this in⋯

I've been battered and scorned

Talked about and torn,

Betrayed by friends, slapped around by men,

But, I'm still here!

I've been tried by rape, told I was a mistake.

Labeled with shame, I even answered to blame.

But, look at me, I'm still here!

I've been doped up and cracked out.

I've even given prostitution a shout.

I've been tested, arrested, even molested

Branded a liar because of the fire,

But, Dearest God, I'm still here!

I've been through the fire.

I've walked through the flood.

I've been sinking in the mire.

But, Lord, I recall the blood!

I was messed up, beat up, and dirty with sin.

But, I remember Madea told me, you'd take me in.

Lord, here I am with no place to go.

I'm asking for help, please don't tell me no.

Pain's been my companion, death ever so near,

But God, you must have something for me

Because I am still here!

I'm still here and so are you.

Our purpose continues to persist.

God is still near.

My Beloved, whether man, woman, boy, or girl, there's a reason you are still here.

God's provided this awesome plan for you to know who you are, what you are, and why you are here.

You are a spirit housed in a body living on earth to impact the world with your kingdom assignment.

God placed in you to be released in your sphere of influence to manifest His glory so everyone can know the real you and Him.

It's time to release yourself into your divine purpose because people are waiting on you.

You must be free to be your true self.

You may still feel trapped, right now.

But, your right now is not your "will be".

Whether self-imprisoned, enslaved by others or your own choices, handcuffed to ideals, chained to wrong motives, strapped to deadly mindsets, locked into religion, blocked by folks, hung up on traditions, curled up in depression, sleeping in pity, walking in doubt, sitting in shame, laying in adultery, caught in homosexuality, grasped by fear, yoked by fornication, harangued by pride, a kinsman to envy, related to jealousy, betrothed to greed, a CEO, janitor, bus driver, author, rich, poor, middle-class, destitute, living in the White House or the crack house, shopping at Sears or

Saks, working at Wal-Mart or on Wall Street, driving a Benz or riding a bus, styling Gucci or still wearing Guess, classified a sinner or saved, a junkie or jailed, you are the guard overseeing your prison.

You have the key on the inside of you to free yourself.

Open the gate.

Come out.

May I ask you a question?

Why are you still a prisoner?

Why are you waiting on someone to free you when Jesus already placed the keys in your hands?

Swing the doors open, release yourself proclaiming to the world, "I am free. I am FREE TO BE...ME."

I know who I am—spirit.

I know what I am—filled with purpose and the assignments attached.

I know why I exist—my arrival on earth was a divine manifestation of God, which destined me to be here at this moment, in this time, for such a time as this so my purpose can be released.

I am an essential part of God's kingdom to carry out my purpose and assignments in a manner that no one else can ever do, which makes me free—*FREE to BE...ME.*

The New King James Version of the bible is used for scriptures contained in this book.

Author Cristi R. Williams is available for speaking engagements,

Contact information:

Facebook Fan Page: Free To Be...Me Cristi Renea

f2bmeauthor@yahoo.com

504.23F-2F2BME

504.233.2263

Made in the USA
Charleston, SC
25 July 2016